SCRIPTURAL HOLINESS AND KESWICK TEACHING COMPARED

Rev. A. M. Hills, B.A., B.D., D.D.

Author of
Backsliders and Worldly Christians
The Cleansing Baptism
Dying to Live
The Establishing Grace
Fundamental Christian Theology
Holiness and Power
Homiletics and Pastoral Theology
Life of Charles G. Finney

SCHMUL PUBLISHING COMPANY
NICHOLASVILLE, KENTUCKY

This Schmul Publishing Co. edition is not a scanned facsimile of a used book. It has not been "updated" or edited into modern English, punctuation or grammar, but is accurate to the author's own style and usage. The text has been carefully proofread for accuracy and formatted for easier reading by today's readers. Every effort has been made to prevent disordered text.

Published by Schmul Publishing Co.
PO Box 776
Nicholasville, KY 40340
USA

Printed in the United States of America

ISBN 10: 0-88019-631-9
ISBN 13: 978-0-88019-631-4

Visit us on the Internet at www.wesleyanbooks.com, or order direct from the publisher by calling 800-772-6657, or by writing to the above address.

Contents

Dedication.

To the precious Christian hearts and the truly devout souls who long for God's best and in whom the Holy Spirit has awakened a craving for inward purity, the holiness which God commands and "the sanctification without which no man shall see the Lord," and who have not yet found the way to reach the blessing, this book is lovingly dedicated by

THE AUTHOR.

Foreword.

WITHIN THE LAST HALF-CENTURY a movement towards the deepening of the spiritual life has sprung up, born of the Spirit-wrought desire in thousands of Christian people for a life of real deliverance from sin.

This movement stands divided into two sections, each having the same desire— to know all that may be known while down here upon earth of God's power to save from sin— but differing widely in their conception of the extent of that power to us-ward while we remain in the body.

One section, which has become identified with the name "Keswick," declares that sin must remain in us to the last day of our life, but that the grace of God provides a "divine counteraction" for it, to quote their own phrase.

On the other hand stand arrayed a great body of earnest souls, including, so far as their avowed doctrines are concerned, the Methodist Church, the Salvation Army, and a great number of holiness people both in and outside of the churches. These declare that, according to Scripture, the death of Jesus Christ provided for the crucifixion of the old man, and that we may claim and experience the destruction here and now of the body of sin.

In this book Dr. Hills first states with great clearness the position of those who, along with men of earlier times, such as George Fox the sanctified Quaker, John Fletcher the saintly Church of England clergyman, John Wesley the great founder of Methodism, and many others, stand for the cleansing of the heart from all sin through the baptism with the Holy Ghost and fire.

He then examines the Keswick position, ascertained by the careful perusal of numerous reports of addresses delivered at Keswick, and published year by year in a volume entitled "Keswick Week," and seeks to point out with great fairness the flaws in this position.

Some people have expressed a fear lest this book should be considered uncharitable and should therefore do harm. We freely admit that such discussions may be carried on in an uncharitable spirit; when it is so, they defeat their own ends. But such a spirit is not necessary.

The present comparison of Keswick Teaching with Scriptural Holiness is made in the spirit of brotherly love; its sole object is to clear away difficulties and errors, and to help souls into a better experience than the teaching of the "counteraction of sin" usually leads them to.

E. K. CROSSLEY.
M. A. HATCH.

Part 1.
Scriptural Holiness Teaching

Chapter I.
Definitions.

When thoughtful and candid people widely disagree on a subject of common interest, nothing so facilitates discussion as careful attention to definitions. There must be some proper sense in which common terms are used. Words must have some definite and assignable meaning, some admitted usage, so that they convey clear ideas to intelligent people. Otherwise speech is useless and argument is impossible.

In such a discussion as this upon which we now enter it is pertinent to ask, What does the New Testament teach? What idea does it convey by the words— sin, repentance, regeneration, the carnal mind, holiness, sanctification, sanctify, sanctified, cleansed, pure?

These and many similar terms we do well to examine carefully, critically, if we would get at the mind of God and the teaching of His inspired Word. Carelessness here will keep us from arriving at the truth by which Jesus prayed that we might be sanctified. May the Holy Spirit guide us and instruct us as we write these coming pages!

Let us consider, then, the meaning of

1. Sin.

A standard commentator of widely recognised ability and scholarship, Dr. Adam Clarke, says: "Sin exists in the soul after two modes or forms: (1) In GUILT, which requires *forgiveness* or *pardon;* (2) in POLLUTION, which requires *cleansing.*

GUILT, to be forgiven, must be *confessed;* POLLUTION, to be cleansed, must be also *confessed.* In order to find *mercy* a man must know and feel himself to be a sinner, that he may fervently apply to God for pardon; but in order to get *a clean heart* a man must know and feel its depravity, acknowledge and deplore it before God, in order to be fully sanctified."

Now, does the New Testament usage warrant Dr. Clarke's double definition of the word "sin"? It certainly does. A Greek lexicon of the New Testament lies before me. The first three definitions of the most common word for sin in the New Testament are these: "Error, offence, sin." Unquestionably this refers to the actual, voluntary sins which men consciously commit. It means transgressions, iniquities, and is usually used in the plural number, as in I. John i. 9: "If we confess our *sins,* He is faithful and just to forgive us our *sins.*" Forgiveness, pardon, deals with this form of sin. We get pardon for sins in justification. Justification may be defined as that judicial act of God by which, on condition of the sinner's repentance and faith in the atoning Saviour, He pardons his sins, remits the penalty, restores him to the Divine favour, and treats him as if he had never sinned.

But the next three definitions of sin in this Greek lexicon are: "A *principle* or *cause* of sin, *proneness* to sin, sinful *propensity.*" In this sense the word is used in the singular number, as in I. John i. 7: "The blood of Jesus Christ His Son cleanseth us from all sin." The word means here what we mean in popular speech by the word "depravity" and "carnality."

Now, the reader will observe that this form of sin is not *pardoned,* like the other kind of sin. It was born in us. It did not come by any act of will of ours. We are not primarily responsible for having it, any more than we are responsible for having a nose, or two ears, or two eyes. We cannot, therefore, be pardoned for it; but, as the above text says, "The blood of Jesus Christ *cleanseth* us from it," whenever we accept such an operation of grace. That is just what we need. It is a most troublesome thing in our moral being, this "proneness," this "propensity" to sin. It makes it hard for us to do right, and please God and love Him with all our hearts, and our neighbours as ourselves. It also makes it very easy to do wrong, easy to backslide, easy to give place to unholy anger, pride, envy, jealousy, covetousness, and the gratification of evil appetites. It is a disposition of insubordination within us, an evil, abnormal appetite for some form of sin, always seeking expression in some form of activity.

This unnatural inclination to evil is what gives so much trouble to Christians. It lies in wait for them continually. It stirs within them evil desires after forbidden things. It makes them amazed at themselves. They know they love God, yet they are conscious of something within them at war with that love. They know they hate sin, and have repented of it and turned away from it. Yet all the same, they often feel within them a startling attraction for it and an inclination to commit it. They are conscious that their bosoms do not glow as they should with the fervours of piety and devotion. They sadly sing—

"O for a closer walk with God,
A calm and heavenly frame!"

Why do they not have that closer walk and heavenly frame? It is this indwelling sin that robs them of their peace and keeps them from the longed-for intimacy with God. But they sing on—

"Where is the blessedness I knew
   When first I saw the Lord?
Where is that soul-refreshing view
   Of Jesus and His Word?
What peaceful hours I then enjoyed!
   How sweet their memory still!
But now I find an aching void
   The world can never fill."

Now, what drove away the blessedness of their primal Christian experience? What produced that aching void in their hearts? It is what the Apostle was complaining of when he wrote: "It is no more I, but *the* SIN *dwelling in me."* It is this "SIN dwelling in" the believer after regeneration that so often makes havoc of the religious life, that defeats the holy purposes, and clouds the hopes and nullifies the vows and blights the aspirations and withers the joys of the poor struggling Christian who still pants for God as the hart pants for the waterbrooks.

This is no private theory of mine. This is the theology of the ages. Dr. Charles Hodge, the prince of Calvinistic theologians in America, wrote: "According to Scripture and the undeniable evidence of history, regeneration does not remove all sin." But *actual, voluntary* sin was pardoned in justification and regeneration, as all theologians teach. It must, then, be this second form of "indwelling sin" which Dr. Hodge says is left in us after regeneration.

Dr. Steven Tyng, of New York City, said to his communicants: "Though truly a child of God, you still carry with you a heart far from sanctified, a remaining SINFULNESS OF NATURE in its appetites and propensities."

In other words, this great Episcopalian theologian affirms that it is this "propensity" form of sin that is left in us after regeneration which SANCTIFICATION removes.

The Presbyterian Confession of Faith says: "When God converts a sinner... He freeth him from his natural bondage under sin; yet by reason of HIS REMAINING CORRUPTION he doth not yet perfectly and only will that which is good, but doth also will that which is evil.

In other words, this creed says it is this REMAINING CORRUPTION, this internal form of *sin,* that is left after regeneration that makes the Christian life so unsteady and inconsistent.

This is also taught by the Church of England: "AND THIS INFECTION OF NATURE doth remain, yea in them that are regenerated... This lust hath in itself the *nature of* SIN."

In perfect harmony with the above, John Wesley taught: "The position that there is no sin in a believer, no bent to backsliding, no carnal mind, is thus contrary to the Word of God, so it is to the experience of His children. They feel a heart bent to backsliding, a NATURAL TENDENCY *to evil."*

John Wesley and his helpers set for themselves the task of offering to the Church of God a cure for this second form of sin, this natural TENDENCY TO EVIL that remains after regeneration.

This second form of sin is designated and described in different ways in the Bible, so that we shall not fail to recognise it and understand the importance of getting rid of it.

In Rom. vi. 6 it is personified, and called "the old man."

In Rom. vii. 17 it is again personified, and called "sin that dwelleth in me," as if there were in the soul-house a hostile inmate called "sin," a spirit of disobedience.

In Rom. vii. 23 it is called "the LAW of sin." If for the word "law" we substitute "a uniform tendency," which is its meaning, we shall get a flood of light upon the evil thing. It is the strange spirit of the devil put into every child by race inheritance, a UNIFORM TENDENCY to do wrong and run after sin and run away from God.

In Rom. viii. 2 the figure is intensified, and it is called

"the law of sin and death" (the *uniform tendency* to sin and death), as if this evil thing were like Asiatic leprosy which makes no truce and works on and on until it brings its victim at last down to death.

In Rom. viii. 7 it is called "the carnal mind which is enmity against God." "It is not subject to the law of God, neither indeed can be." It cannot be pacified, or placated, or reconciled or won over into friendship with God. It is first and last and always a bitter enemy to all holiness in us, because it hates God's law and God Himself.

What an awful thing it is for a Christian to knowingly and voluntarily harbour in his heart such a malignant enemy of his loving Lord!

In Heb. xii. 15 this evil thing is called "a root of bitterness." If allowed to remain in us it may grow up any time into envy, jealousy, hatred, or revenge, and destroy all the peace and piety of the heart.

In Heb. xii. 1 it is called "the sin that doth so easily beset us." This hints at some evil, treacherous, slimy thing that is always lying in wait for us, ready at any unexpected moment to spring on us and destroy our souls.

In Heb. iii. 12 it is called "an evil heart of unbelief in departing from the living God." It is this indwelling sin, this satanic traitor in the heart, that prompts Christians to suspicion Christ, and question His grace, and cast reflections upon His love, and disbelieve His promises of guidance and salvation.

Think of it! Our patient, beloved Jesus is compelled to bear it through long weary years, while we, His blood-bought ones, toy with this form of sin in our inmost souls. Oh, the matchless grace of our Saviour, that would brook such insult and wait so long for us to permit the Holy Spirit to put out this evil proclivity to sin and Satan and hell!

2. Repentance.

One of our greatest American theologians defines repentance as follows:— "Evangelical repentance is called a 'repentance toward God,' because it consists in turning *from sin* TO HOLINESS, implying a sense and hatred of sin and a love of holiness."

This is a most suggestive and Scriptural definition. The Bible pictures of repentance are very striking. One says: "O my God, I am *ashamed* and *blush* to lift up my face to Thee, my God" (Ezra ix. 6).

Another says: "Wherefore, I *abhor myself,* and repent in dust and ashes" (Job xlii. 6).

Another wrote: "Then shall ye remember your evil ways, and *loathe* yourselves." (Ezek. xxxvi. 31).

Another exclaimed: "For I *acknowledge* my transgression, and my sin is ever before me." (Ps. li. 3).

Another commanded: "Repent and turn yourselves from your idols, and turn away your faces from all your abominations."

Another wrote: "If we confess our sins, He is faithful and just to forgive us" (I. John i. 9).

Ex. xxii. 3: "The thief shall make restitution."

These various passages show what Scriptural repentance is. It means such an abhorrence of evil, and such a self-loathing on account of it— yea, such a confession of it and a forsaking of it— as implies a real going out of the sin business. God says: "Let the wicked forsake his way, and the unrighteous man his thoughts" (Is. lv. 7). "Repent, and turn yourselves from your idols, and turn away your faces from all your abominations."

It is no easy experience. It means a tremendous overhauling of the moral life, and a going out of partnership with Satan and sin. It implies making confession to God and men, a thorough righting of wrongs, and a change of front of the spiritual being. He who consented to sin, and pursued after it and revelled in it, now abhors that wicked past from his inmost soul, and turns himself in the opposite direction towards God and holiness.

It is safe to say that a person who has passed through such an experience thoroughly will not again trifle carelessly with sin. Neither will he speak lightly of holiness. Above all, he will not oppose holiness. He will instinctively feel that it would be a help to him. He would welcome it as a God-send, or anything else that would hold him back from the repetition of his wretched sins.

3. What is Regeneration?

The following definition of regeneration is taken from a Methodist Theology widely used in the United States. It is the belief and teaching of our preachers of holiness:—

"Regeneration is that moral change in man wrought by the Holy Spirit, by which he is saved from the love of sin, the practice of sin, and the dominion of sin, and is enabled, with full choice of will and the energy of right affections, to love God and to keep His commandments."

It will be seen from the above definition that regeneration is not

(a) The result of water-baptism, nor is it caused by it.

(b) It is not a mere reformation wrought by the human will. It is the work of God.

In regeneration, through the Holy Spirit's influence, there is the constitution of a new and holy choice which leads to a new character, loyal to God and duty.

He who is regenerated no longer loves sin, and no longer knowingly commits it. He obeys the known will of God, and keeps pace with the light given to his soul. To refuse to do so would be to forfeit his grace and lose his experience.

"Whosoever is begotten of God doeth no sin, because His seed abideth in him, and he cannot sin (and still keep regenerated) because he is begotten of God" (I. John iii.9).

The literal meaning of the Greek tenses is: "He that hath been born of God, and continues to be so, is not doing sin."

We can explain it in this simple way. A total abstainer cannot get drunk and still be a total abstainer. An honest man cannot constantly steal and retain his honesty. A truthful man cannot practise lying and retain his truthfulness. And so, says God, a regenerated person cannot commit sin and retain His grace. The new birth goes entirely against sin. The experience commits a man against practising sin and lifts him spiritually above the sin level.

We have to surrender all known sin to get born of God, and it costs the same to keep the experience. When, under the convicting influence of the Spirit of God, we repented and sought regeneration, we gave up *expecting* to sin. We wanted to be done with all rebellion against our Heavenly Father. We *did* give it up in our purpose, once and for all.

Now, notice that thereafter the whole moral attitude of a true child of God will be changed. He hates what he once loved, and loves what he once hated. When a man becomes converted the onlooking world expects a change in him, and it has a right to. As a child advertises his family and resembles his parent, so to be born of God is to resemble God in all that is visible to men— the outward life. When a man who professes to be a Christian wantonly sins, people are both horrified and disgusted. It is the instinctive judgment of people that his life is inconsistent with his profession. The cold, critical world expects Christians to live without committing sin, and sneers at them if they do not.

Notice further: "Whosoever abideth in Him sinneth not" (I. John iii. 6). "Whosoever is begotten of God doeth no sin, because His seed abideth in him: and he cannot sin, because he is begotten of God (verse 9).

In other words, while the regeneration seed remains in

a soul, his antagonism to sin keeps up. "He cannot sin": it is not a natural "cannot," but a moral "cannot." While the principle of honesty remains in a man he cannot be dishonest; he must first surrender his principle before he can cheat his neighbour. So the first *wilful* sin unjustifies us, and the seed of regeneration is taken away. Before we can consent to the evil deed we must previously surrender our saving grace. When we are below "not committing sin," we are living below a Christian experience.

(1) *It follows from the above that there is no such thing as habitually sinning Christians.* There is an old catechism that asks: "Is any man able perfectly to keep the commandments of God? "

It answers: "No man is able, either of himself or by any grace received in this life, to keep the commandments of God, but doth daily break them in thought, word and deed."

Dr. Adam Clarke remarks upon this monstrous statement: "The devil cannot sin daily in more ways than that." A friend of mine, one of our holiness evangelists, pertinently asks: "If a Christian can sin daily in thought, word, and deed, and go to heaven, what would one have to do to go to hell?"

The only answer we need to give to such a creed-statement as that is the oath of God Almighty: "The oath which He sware unto Abraham our father, to grant unto us that we, being delivered out of the hand of our enemies, should serve Him without fear, in holiness and righteousness before Him all our days" (Luke i. 73-75). Evidently God never planned for a species of "sinning Christians" in His economy of grace. He plainly tells us that while we keep our regenerating grace we will not, cannot sin.

(2) It follows further that *a justified and regenerated man is under obligation to live just as well outwardly as a sanctified or holy man.* There are no two standards of living.

Perfect obedience to all known duty is the standard for every moral being in the universe. God cannot tolerate sinning in anyone. We must each walk in whatever light we have, and obey God. A sanctified man can do no more outwardly, and a justified, regenerated man can do no less, and keep saved.

(3) I may observe in closing that *this outward obedience to the known will of God is what some teachers hold up as the* EXPERIENCE OF HOLINESS. The whole drift of their sermons shows that this is their conception of it. But this is not the teaching of Scripture.

Obedience to God in outward conduct is refraining from actual sin, voluntary sin, the first form of sin. But that is not Bible holiness or sanctification. By itself it is only the experience of justification and regeneration.

4. What is Sanctification or Holiness?

These terms are synonymous. In the Authorised Version of the New Testament the same Greek noun was translated five times holiness and five times sanctification. In the New Version it is every time translated sanctification. Our English lexicons show that they are synonymous terms. The same Greek adjective is the root of the noun sanctification and the noun translated holiness. For brevity of discussion we may treat them as one. Holiness is sanctification. What is that?

(1) Webster's Dictionary defines it as:

"The ACT OF God's grace by which the affections of men are PURIFIED or alienated from sin and the world, and exalted to a supreme love to God; also THE STATE OF BEING THUS PURIFIED."

(2) The Century Dictionary defines it thus:

"In theology, the ACT OF GOD'S GRACE by which the affections of men are purified and the soul is CLEANSED from sin and consecrated to God… Conformity of heart and life to the will of God."

(3) Worcester's Dictionary:

Sanctify: (1) To FREE FROM THE POWER OF SIN; TO CLEANSE FROM CORRUPTION; to make holy. Sanctification: the ACT of sanctifying or PURIFYING from the dominion of sin. (2) The act of consecrating or setting apart to a sacred end or office."

(4) Standard Dictionary:

"Sanctify: To make holy; render sacred; morally or spiritually pure; CLEANSED FROM SIN. Sanctification— specifically in theology— the GRACIOUS WORK of the Holy Spirit whereby the BELIEVER IS FREED FROM SIN and exalted to HOLINESS OF HEART AND LIFE."

The thoughtful, critical reader will no doubt notice a surprising agreement in these definitions. The reason evidently is that the lexicographers were scholarly men who were honestly defining words. They were not riding any theological hobbies. They were not trying to agree with or disagree with any theory of any class of men whatsoever. They were simply defining words. They all clearly assert:

(*a*) That sanctification is wrought in us by God, and three of them say by an "ACT OF GOD." This rules out all slow process and the "get-it-by-growth" theory. God puts forth His acts instantaneously, and that is the way He brings sanctification to the life.

(*b*) Four of them distinctly assert that it is a PURIFYING, CLEANSING work, by which the soul is "CLEANSED FROM SIN."

(*c*) One of them says it is the work of THE HOLY SPIRIT, the Third Person of the Trinity. The others do not disagree with this, but use the more general term "God." Let us remember, then, that as they and the Scriptures affirm, it is the specific work of the Holy Spirit to sanctify.

(*d*) One of them affirms distinctly that it is only "BELIEVERS" who are thus cleansed from sin, persons "who are already IN JESUS," and "UNITED TO HIM BY FAITH." The others say nothing to the contrary. Now that rules out the "*get-it-all-at-conversion*" theory. It establishes a distinct, epochal SECOND WORK OF GRACE.

(*e*) These lexicographers all use phrases of similar import, "cleansed from," "purified from," "freed from sin." All these phrases in combination distinctly teach the ERADICATION of indwelling sin and NOT THE SUPPRESSION of it. They teach deliverance from it. It is very important for the reader to bear these distinctions carefully in mind, for we have a class of so-called holiness teachers who deny every one of these truths.

Now let us hear from the theologians and the well-known holiness teachers on this subject. Dr. John Owen said: "To be cleansed from the defilements of sin, whatever they be; to have a heart inclined, disposed, enabled to fear the Lord always and to walk in all His ways and statutes accordingly, with an internal, habitual conformity of the whole soul unto the law of God, is to be SANCTIFIED or HOLY."

Wesley wrote: "Both my brother Charles and I maintain that Christian perfection is that love of God and our neighbour which implies DELIVERANCE FROM ALL SIN." "It is the loving God with all our heart, mind, soul and strength. This implies that no wrong temper, none contrary to love, remains in the soul; and that all the thoughts, words and actions are governed by pure love." "Certainly sanctification (in the proper sense) is an INSTANTANEOUS DELIVERANCE FROM ALL SIN."

Notice, during the different years of Wesley's life, what terms he used to express it.

1739. "Renewal of our heart after the image of God." "The mind that was in Christ."

1741. "Deliverance from inward and outward sin." "The evil nature, the body of sin destroyed."

1742. "Cleansed from all the filth of self and pride." "To perfect health restored." "To sin entirely dead."

1757. "Having received the first fruits of the Spirit, patiently and earnestly wait for the great change whereby every 'root of bitterness' may be torn up."

1758. "A heart entirely pure." "Perfected in love and saved from all sin."

1761. "Delivered from the root of bitterness." "Cleansed from all unrighteousness." "After being convinced of inbred sin, in a moment they feel all faith and love, no pride, self-will, or anger."

1762. Full renewal in the image of God." "In an instant emptied of all sin and filled with God." "An instantaneous deliverance from all sin." "Cleansed from sin, meaning all sinful tempers."

1763. "The second blessing." "Destruction of the roots of sin in one moment" "Pure love."

1765. "Love taking up the whole heart, and filling it with all holiness." "The soul pure from every spot, clean from all unrighteousness." Sin destroyed in a moment."

1768. "The image of God stamped on the heart." "The mind that was in Christ, enabling us to walk as Christ walked" "The perfection I have taught these forty years." "I mean loving God with all our heart and our neighbour as ourselves. I pin down all opposers to this definition; no evasion; no shifting the question."

1770. "An entire deliverance from sin and recovery of the whole image of God." "A second change, whereby we shall be saved from all sin and perfected in love."

1774. "The second blessing, properly so-called, deliverance from the root of bitterness, from inbred as well as actual sin."

1781. "Christ in a pure and sinless heart, reigning the Lord of every motion."

1785. "A full deliverance from all sin and a renewal in the whole image of God." "Full salvation now by simple faith.

1789. "The whole image of God wherein you were created." "O be satisfied with nothing less and you will surely secure it by simple faith."

Plainly Mr. Wesley had no idea of what has been called the "suppression" theory— the evil nature being kept down by dominant grace in the heart. His idea of full sanctification was COMPLETE DELIVERANCE FROM INWARD AND OUTWARD SIN.

Dr. Adam Clarke: "What, then, is this complete sanctification? It is the cleansing by the Blood of that which has not been cleansed; it is washing the soul of a true believer from the remains of sin."

Rev. John Fletcher: "It is the pure love of God and man shed abroad in a faithful believer's heart by the Holy Ghost given unto him, to *cleanse* him and to *keep him clean* from all the FILTHINESS of the *flesh and spirit.*"

Rev. Joseph Benson: "To sanctify you wholly is to complete the work of PURIFICATION and renovation begun in your regeneration."

Binney: "Entire sanctification is that act of the Holy Spirit whereby the JUSTIFIED SOUL is made holy."

On these definitions J. A. Wood remarks: "Much of the prejudice and opposition to this doctrine come from remaining depravity in unsanctified believers. Indwelling sin is an antagonism to holiness, and, in so far as any Christian has inbred sin, he has within him opposition to holiness. Many do not yield to it, but resist it, pray against it and keep it under; others, we are sorry to know, both in the ministry and laity, yield to their depravity, and stand in opposition to God's work."

We are now prepared to give a formal definition of sanctification or Scriptural holiness, which would probably be accepted by the three hundred teachers and preachers in the National Holiness Association of America, and by the holiness teachers in the Salvation Army, and by Methodist advocates of holiness.

ENTIRE SANCTIFICATION IS A SECOND DEFINITE WORK OF

GRACE WROUGHT BY THE BAPTISM WITH THE HOLY SPIRIT IN THE HEART OF THE BELIEVER SUBSEQUENTLY TO REGENERATION, RECEIVED INSTANTANEOUSLY BY FAITH, BY WHICH THE HEART IS CLEANSED FROM ALL INWARD CORRUPTION AND FILLED WITH THE PERFECT LOVE OF GOD.

Let us now discuss this blessing more fully.

(1) *Sanctification is more "than deliverance from the committal of sins.* To be kept continually from wilful sins is not peculiar to sanctification. Regeneration, as described by the Scripture, we have seen, does all that. The grace of God implanted in all at conversion is strong enough to give us constant victory over every temptation. But this is below the state we are now considering.

(2) *Sanctification is also deliverance from the existence of* INDWELLING SIN. The "old man" is crucified, and the "body of sin" is done away (Rom. vi. 6). The sinful disposition is purged away (Is. i. 25), or removed by the refining fire of the Holy Spirit (Mal. iii. 3). Entire sanctification is a state of being *cleansed from all sin,* even INDWELLING SIN, called depravity (I. John i. 7).

(3) Again, *sanctification is even more than cleansing from all sin. That is only the negative side of the blessing.* But there is also a positive side to it. It is being "filled with the Spirit" (Eph. v. 18). This brings love in its fulness and power for service. "The love of God hath been shed abroad in our hearts through the Holy Spirit" (Rom. v. 5). "Ye shall receive power when the Holy Spirit is come upon you" (Acts i. 8). Sanctification is a great experience. It means the purity of believers and the Church, and the unwonted progress of the Kingdom of Jesus Christ.

Chapter II.
Why We Teach a Second Blessing.

THE MODERN CHURCH WAS TAUGHT this by God Himself. About 1757 there broke out what has been called the second great Methodist revival. The peculiarity was that it was a revival among *believers,* an outpouring of the Spirit upon those who were *already regenerated* and living *in Christ.* It did not seem to come about through the design or the efforts of any single preacher, for it broke out simultaneously in various parts of England. Christians here and there began to enter into the enjoyment of a *conscious full salvation from sin.*

On March 12th, 1760, John Wesley wrote of many such: "It is plain:—

"(1) They feel no *inward sin* and, to the best of their knowledge, they commit no outward sin.

"(2) They see and love God every moment, and pray, rejoice and give thanks evermore.

"(3) They have constantly as clear a witness from God of sanctification as they have of justification. Now in this I do rejoice and will rejoice, call it what you please; and I would to God thousands had experienced thus much. Let them afterward experience as much as God pleases."

July 29th, 1761, Wesley wrote of his Christian members: "Many have and many do daily experience an unspeakable change. After being deeply convinced of inbred sin, particularly of pride, anger, self-will and unbelief, in a moment they feel all faith and love, no pride, no self-will or anger; and from that moment they have continual fellowship with God, always rejoicing, praying and giving thanks. Whoever ascribes such a change to the devil, I ascribe it to the Spirit of God."

Such examples as these of well-known Christians of an unquestioned experience of salvation, always foremost in piety and good works in their several communities, entering suddenly into another epochal experience of salvation, a deeper work of grace, led Wesley and those who have come after him to study anew and most critically God's method of saving men. We find and teach that there are two separate and perfectly distinct works of grace. The first work of conversion and regeneration does not do for the soul all that needs to be done. As the Ninth Article of the Church of England says: "*This infection of nature* doth remain, yea, in them that are regenerate, whereby the *lust of the flesh* is not subject to the law of God." ["]...This lust hath in itself *the nature of sin.*"

Now everything in us that is unlike God and of the nature of sin must be taken out of us before we are fitted for heaven. Hence the need of a second work of grace. The Bible gives us many examples of such a work, clear and unquestionable. We find that "Abram believed God and it was counted to him for righteousness (Gen. xv. 6). But about twenty years afterwards he got a call to a second blessing of holiness (Gen. xvii. 1). His name was changed to Abraham, to indicate a change in his life. A rite was given to typify it, explained in Col. ii. 11 as signifying "the putting off of his old sinful nature.

We find Jacob had his Peniel and Bethel experiences and a change of name to indicate his changed life.

We find David, after he knew that he was forgiven, praying for sanctification (Ps. li. 7).

Isaiah had been a prophet for years, his heart glowing with the fervour of deep piety. But in the sixth chapter we find him convicted for holiness and getting the experience, not gradually by a slow process of growth, but *suddenly,* in one hour of prayer and communion with God.

In Mal. iii. 3 we read that the "sons of Levi" are to be purified by refining fire. They were the priestly tribe that ministered before the Lord continually; but even they needed the cleansing of fire to offer to the Lord an offering in righteousness. In Mal. iv. 3 a second blessing was promised to them who already feared the Lord.

In Matt. iii. 11 John declared that he indeed baptized with water, the initiatory rite of a religious life, but that Jesus should baptize with the Holy Spirit and fire. It is this fiery baptism which brings the cleansing needed. In the upper chamber, on the night before His crucifixion, Jesus prayed for those who were then His disciples. They had "forsaken all" to follow Him. They had been preaching for three years and casting out devils or demons in the name of the Lord. He said in His prayer: "Thou gavest them to Me, and they have kept Thy word." "They have received My words, and know of a truth that I came forth from Thee, and they believed that Thou didst send Me." "I pray not for the world, but for those whom Thou hast given Me; for they are Thine." "I have given them Thy word; and the world hated them because they are not of the world, even as I am not of the world." He had just given them the communion of the Lord's Supper. He had just said: "I am the Vine, ye are the branches; already ye are clean because of the word which I have spoken unto you." "Abide ye in My love." "Ye did not choose Me, but I chose you and appointed you that ye should go and bear fruit." "If ye were of the world, the world would love its own; but because ye are not of the world, but I chose you out of the world, therefore the world hateth you."

If these words of Jesus in that upper chamber are not a description of true Christian disciples, what words could describe a Christian? And yet afterward, in the same assembly, on the same occasion, in the same prayer, He prayed: *"Sanctify them."* If this was not praying for a second work of grace to be wrought in a disciple of Christ after his regeneration, then the language of Jesus is painfully indefinite and brings confusion of thought to seeking souls.

But there is so much Scripture evidence that we are sure of our footing here. The prayer of Jesus for the sanctification of His disciples was answered at Pentecost. They were immediately *cleansed* from the pride and self-seeking and cowardice and impatience that had characterised their former lives, and they became marvels of Holy Spirit power, as well as holy living, from that very hour.

Philip went down to the city of Samaria and had a gracious revival, and "there was much joy in that city." A good revival of religion always brings joy to a community. A large number were baptised in the Name of Jesus. As soon as the Church of Jerusalem heard of it, they immediately despatched unto them Peter and John, who prayed for them that they might receive the Holy Spirit. And the cleansing Spirit came upon them (Acts viii. 4-17).

Cornelius was "a devout man," who "feared God with all his house" — that is, he had a godly household. "He gave much alms and prayed to God always," and had a vision and a visit from an angel of God. "His prayer was heard and his alms were had in remembrance in the sight of God" (Acts x. 31). He worked righteousness and was acceptable to God (v. 35). He was not an unevangelised heathen, for he had heard the Gospel before (Acts x. 36, 37).

If I wanted to have a delightfully pleasant time in this world, I would like to be pastor of a large Church of as good and godly people as Cornelius and his household. But still God took great pains to have Peter go and preach to them, and they received the baptism with the Spirit. And what it did for them, Peter, years afterward, informed the Council in Jerusalem; "and God, Which knoweth the heart, bare them witness, giving them the Holy Ghost, even as He did unto us; and He made no distinction between us and them, CLEANSING THEIR HEARTS BY FAITH" (Acts xv. 8, 9, R.V.). This is incontrovertible evidence of the method by which God *cleanses* us of the "pollution remaining after regeneration" and thus sanctifies the heart.

Paul, years afterward, found a young body of disciples at Ephesus. His first question was whether they had received the Holy Spirit (Acts xix. 2). Their preacher had not told them that the Spirit was given, just as multitudes of preachers to-day do not seek this baptism, and nobody gets it under their ministry. Hence nobody becomes sanctified, and the Church members are ready to rise up in arms against anybody who preaches this precious doctrine of a second work of grace. But Paul led these disciples right into the experience. It was doubtless to this part of the Church at Ephesus that he refers when he wrote (Eph. i. 13), "After that ye believed ye were sealed with the Holy Spirit of promise."

We are sure we are not mistaken in our interpretation, but are confirmed in it by the letters to the Churches. Every command and call to sanctification in the New Testament is given to *believers only,* people who are already *in Christ*. Such a command is never laid upon sinners. Every *prayer,* for sanctification is prayed in behalf of the members of the Church. It is believers only who are *called* to the blessing. It is wrought in us by the Holy Spirit, "Whom the world cannot receive." It was for the *Church* that "Jesus gave Himself that He might *sanctify* it, having *cleansed* it, that He might present the Church to Himself a glorious Church, not having spot or wrinkle or any such thing, but that it should be holy and without blemish["] (Eph. v. 26, 27, R.V.). Paul longed to get to the Church at Rome that he might impart unto it a spiritual gift (Rom. i. 11), and he was minded to reach the Church at Corinth that they "might have a *second grace*" (II. Cor. i. 15, R.V. m, [*sic*]).

The examination of a single Epistle of S. Paul will prove to a demonstration what I am saying. He writes to the Thessalonians in his first epistle:—

(1) Unto the Church in the Lord Jesus Christ.

(2) "We give thanks for you all" (i. 2). No one can suppose he was thanking God for sinners.

(3) He remembered their faith, love and hope (i. 3).

(4) He called them "brethren beloved of God" (i. 4).

(5) He knew of their election (i. 4).

(6) The Gospel came unto them in power and in the Holy Ghost, converting them to God (i. 5).

(7) These Christians had "*much assurance*" (verse 5). They did not guess or presumptuously imagine that they were Christians. They had assurance.

(8) They imitated the Apostle Paul and Jesus" (i. 6). Sinners do not live in that manner.

(9) They had "joy in the Holy Ghost." Sinners never have joy from Him. He convicts them of sin.

(10) They were ensamples to Christians everywhere (i. 7).

(11) They "sounded forth the word of the Lord" everywhere (i. 8). They had such Christian earnestness that they could not be induced to keep still about their faith in Christ.

(12) They had "turned unto God from idols to serve the living and true God" (i. 9).

(13) They were waiting for His Son from heaven (i. 10). No sinners ever do anything of the kind. The last thing they wish is to have Jesus return and summon them to judgment for their sins.

Now here are thirteen unmistakable evidences that Paul was writing to an earnest body of Christians. He sends Timothy to them to see if they had continued in the faith. Timothy returned with the joyful intelligence that they had not backslidden (see iii. 6-9).

Notice now what the apostle wrote to this young Church. He tells them (iii. 10) that he is praying night and day that he may see their faces and may perfect that which was lacking in their faith, "to the end (verse 13), He may establish your hearts unblameable in holiness." They had exercised faith for justification, but he wanted them to exercise faith a second time for holiness. We know we are treading on firm ground here from what immediately follows: *"For,"* says the apostle (iv. 3), "this is the will of God, even your sanctification." *"For* God called us not for uncleanness but to sanctification" (verse 7).

In the next chapter (v. 23) the apostle prays: "And the God of peace Himself sanctify you wholly; and may your spirit and soul and body be preserved entire, without blame... Faithful is He that calleth you (to sanctification), Who also will do it," sanctify you (v. 24). How could a second blessing be taught more strongly or plainly? These excellent Christians of the first chapter are assured that Paul wants their faith to reach out for holiness, for it is God's will that they should be sanctified; for He hath called them to sanctification. And He is faithful to do it for them (v. 24), and if they reject it, they reject not man but God (iv. 8), "Who giveth His Holy Spirit" to accomplish that very work in the soul. These passages are so linked together that no human ingenuity can rationally interpret them to mean other than a call to a *second work of grace,* namely, HOLINESS or SANCTIFICATION.

Chapter III.
Why We Teach the Eradication of Carnality.

"THE MIND OF THE FLESH (the carnal mind) is enmity against God; for it is not subject to the law of God, neither indeed can be; and they that are in the flesh cannot please God" (Rom. viii. 7). The word for "flesh" is "sarx," used in the New Testament 140 times. It sometimes means the human body; sometimes it means human nature, and again humanity. Sometimes it means carnality, as in the above passage and in Gal. v. 19-21, "Now the works of the flesh are manifest, which are these: adultery, fornication, uncleanness, lasciviousness, idolatry, witchcraft, hatred, variance, emulation, wrath, strife, sedition, heresies, envyings, murders, drunkenness, revellings, and such like." The first four sins in this list are physical sins. But it will be noticed that the next eleven sins in the list are purely mental and spiritual sins, having no connection with the body. So the word "flesh" here must refer to that moral derangement of our being which prompts us to sin. We call it in common speech *carnality* or *depravity.*

Depravity is defined by Webster as "perverseness. The

state of being depraved or corrupted; a vitiated state of moral character; general badness of character; wickedness of mind or heart. It denotes an utter vitiation of principle or feeling. Its synonyms are corruption; vitiation; wickedness; vice; contamination; degeneracy." It refers to the trend or tendency to sin born within us. Jesus referred to this same sad, dark something within us which prompts us to evil when He said: "For from within, out of the heart of men, evil thoughts proceed, fornications, thefts, murders, adulteries, covetings, wickednesses, deceit, lasciviousness, an evil eye, railing, pride, foolishness. All these evil things proceed from within." Here again is a list of thirteen forms or manifestations of sin, and only three of them are physical.

We gather from the above facts that there is an inward corruption of being not natural to our race as it was originally created by God. It has permeated our whole being, body, soul and spirit. It is opposed to all godlikeness within us. It is "enmity against God, for it is not subject to the law of God, neither indeed can be. So then they that are in the flesh cannot please God" (Rom. viii. 7, 8). The word "flesh" cannot mean "body" here, for it would be equivalent to saying that no person, while he lived in the body, could please God. But Jesus lived in a body and He pleased God. Enoch walked with God three hundred years, and had the testimony borne to him "that he had been well pleasing to God" (Heb. xi. 5). But it is true that a person with a carnal mind, a proclivity to evil in him, a perverted nature is not wholly pleasing to God.

We have seen in Chapter I. that the second set of definitions of a New Testament word for sin is "A principle or cause of sin; proneness to sin; sinful propensity." This is, to use another Bible phrase, "the sin that dwelleth in me." In popular speech it is called "inbred sin." The phrase means, that we acquired it from Adam, through race connection, as a result of the fall.

Now the question arises, is there deliverance from this indwelling sin, inbred sin, depravity, carnality? No matter what we call this abnormal condition of our moral nature, can we get rid of it? This is a grave question, in the answer to which every member of our race has a profound interest.

We believe it can be got rid of and that ample provision has been made in the atonement of Jesus Christ to meet every necessity of our moral nature. We think so,

I. Because it would be unreasonable to suppose that God would have allowed a moral race to be propagated under conditions in which it could not possibly be pleasing to Him. As God made our first parents they were pleasing to Him. They were made in His own image and He pronounced them "very good." It was superlative praise which Infinite-Wisdom bestowed. But sin marred the image. There is now a foreign element indwelling our nature which is enmity against God; "for it is not subject to the law of God, neither, indeed, can be, and they that are in the flesh (in this sinful condition) cannot please God." Now who will be rash enough to declare that the atonement of Jesus Christ does not provide for the removal from our nature of anything which is displeasing to God? To me the proposition is unthinkable. "To this end was the Son of God manifested that He might destroy the works of the devil." And certainly no achievement of the devil was so disastrous to the human family as the injection into every human life of a spirit of alienation from God, a trend to evil, a tendency to sin. This is the black nest-egg which produces all the satanic brood of sins that were ever committed. This corruption of our nature was Satan's masterpiece. And to say that he could put an evil into us that the cleansing blood of Christ and the fire of the Holy Spirit cannot remove, is to rob God of His supreme glory and to put the crown of Omnipotence upon Satan's head. True piety *shrinks* from so abhorrent a conclusion. Reverence for an Almighty God refuses to accept as conclusive any argument which can logically end in consequences so fatal to the glory of our Infinite Redeemer.

II. We think this taint of nature can be removed because of the meaning of the verbs which God uses with regard to it.

(1) In Ephesians iv. 22 He says "PUT OFF" (apotithimi) the "old man."

(2) In I. John iii. 8 He says: "The Son of God was manifested that He might DESTROY (luo) the works of the devil."

(3) In Rom. vi. 6 we are assured that vision was made in the Atonement for the "old man" to be "CRUCIFIED" (sustoroo).

(4) In the same verse we are told that the "body of sin" might be DESTROYED" (katargeo). The meaning of the word is, "to put an end to," to "annihilate."

(5) In Rom. vi. 18 and vi. 22 He tells us that we can be "SET FREE FROM" sin (eleutheroo).

(6) In Col. ii. 9-11 we are told we can have a spiritual circumcision which consists in the PUTTING OFF (apekdusii) the body of the flesh," meaning the same as the "body of sin" in Rom. vi. 6.

(7) In II. Tim. ii. 21 we are told that if a man purge himself from these (sins) he shall be sanctified. Notice a purged man is a sanctified man. The verb for "purged" (ekkathairo) means "to *cleanse thoroughly,*" "to PURGE OUT," "to ELIMINATE."

(8) In Col. iii. 5 we are told to MORTIFY sin. The verb is nekroo, which means to PUT TO DEATH, to KILL. Ellicott says the aorist tense in the text means, "to KILL AT ONCE."

In the Old Testament we learn the same.

(9) In Isa. i. 25 we learn that the dross of inward sin is to be "taken away" and "PURGED AWAY."

(10) In Ezek. xxxvi. 25 God promises to CLEANSE FROM all filthiness.

(11) In Mal. iii. 3 we are told that God will PURIFY the sons of Levi and PURGE them as gold and silver. The figure is that of purifying precious metals and the verbs mean the separation of the alloy from the gold.

Now, here are twelve verbs in the Old and New Testaments which teach God's method of dealing with this internal, indwelling sin. They all unite in declaring that He will "crucify" it, "kill" it, "destroy" it, "eliminate" it, "burn" it, and "take it away" from the soul. And what is more, no other kind of verbs are used when describing God's method of dealing with this old foe of His dwelling in our hearts. The conclusion is irresistible. God proposes, if we will consent to it, to *cleanse our hearts entirely and free us for ever from this devilish thing within us that constantly tempts us to sin.*

III. We are confirmed in our faith by the meaning of the adjectives which are used. Take the adjective "katharos." Its meanings are "Clean, pure, unsoiled, guiltless, void of evil." It is found in such passages as these: Matt. v. 8, "Blessed are the *pure* in heart;" I. Tim. 1. 5, "Out of a *pure* heart;" I. Tim, iii. 9, "In a *pure* conscience;" II. Tim. ii. 22, "Out of a *pure* heart;" James i. 27, "*Pure* and white linen;" Rev. xxi. 18, "*Pure* gold;" Rev. xxii. 1, "*Pure* river of water."

It is thus seen that it is applied to the heart, the conscience, religion, linen, gold and water. We know these other things can be pure, gold without alloy, water without sediment, linen not mixed with cotton or wool. Why may we not believe then that there can be a conscience cleansed by the blood and a heart made *pure* by the Holy Spirit, and free from the carnal mind?

This adjective is the basis of the verb katharizo, which is used three times in Matt. viii. 2, 3: "And behold there came a leper and worshipped Him, saying, Lord, if Thou wilt, Thou *canst make me clean.* And Jesus put forth His hand and touched him saying, I will; be thou clean. And immediately his leprosy *was cleansed.*" Now, did Jesus really cleanse the leper or only play at it and suppress its outward manifestations, but leave the disease still within to corrupt the body and spread its contagion to others? Fortunately we are not left to any conjecture on this point. Luke v, 13, "Immediately the leprosy *departed* from him."

But this same verb is used in Acts xv. 9, where we are informed that "the Holy Spirit... *cleansed* their hearts by faith." In the light of the use of the verb and the meaning of the adjective, are we not driven to the conclusion that the moral defilement and indwelling sin of the believers was ENTIRELY REMOVED from them by the baptism with the Holy Spirit?

Our conviction that we are right is still further strengthened by another use of this adjective. Remember, it means "clean," "pure," "unsoiled," "upright," "void of evil." It is compounded with the Greek preposition "ek," into another verb ekkathairo. The lexicons give the meanings as, "to CLEANSE OUT," "thoroughly PURIFY," "to PURGE OUT," "to ELIMINATE." It is used in 1. Cor. v. 7: "Purge out the old leaven," and in II. Tim. ii. 21 we are informed that if a man is thus purged from the old leaven of carnality and sins, he is "SANCTIFIED, meet for the Master's use, prepared unto every good work." In four passages we are told that we are *sanctified by the Holy Spirit.* Here, then, are our conclusions:—

(1) We are sanctified by the Spirit.

(2) It is done by the baptism with the Spirit, cleansing our hearts (Acts xv. 8, 9).

(3) It consists of "PURGING OUT" or "ELIMINATING."

(4) It makes us *"pure,"* like "pure water" or *"pure gold"* from which *sediment* or *alloy* has been *"purged out"* or "eliminated," or like an Israelite's tent from which the leaven has been *"purged."* Hallelujah! this is what every Christian heart hungers for, *deliverance* from the carnal mind.

IV. Let us consider the meaning of the Greek adjective "hagios," Its meanings are: (1) "Separate from common use;" (2) "hallowed;" (3) "pure, righteous." It is used about 240 times in the New Testament and in the sense of "pure, righteous," a vast number of times. It is used about a hundred times of God the Father, Son, and Spirit; four times of angels; nineteen times of men and women. We might infer from this that the blood of Christ and the purifying work of the Holy Ghost in our hearts would produce in us a holiness in kind like that in God and the angels, alike free from carnality.

From this adjective is formed the verb "hagiazo," which means, "to consecrate," "to cleanse," "to purify," "to sanctify." This is the verb S. Paul used when he prayed, "And the very God of peace Himself *sanctify* you wholly." (German, "through and through.") "And I pray God your whole spirit and soul and body be preserved blameless." And Jesus used it in His intercessory prayer for His disciples: "Father, sanctify them" (John xvii. 17). For this He died (Eph. v. 26). Is it thinkable that Jesus prayed for nothing higher, and died for nothing better, than to leave the members of His Church a mass of carnality and inward corruption? When the infinite God undertakes to sanctify you, make you "pure through and through," in spirit, soul and body, does He still leave every corner of your being infested with a carnality that is at war with God? Who can believe it for a moment?

The participle of this verb is used in Heb. x. 14: "For by one offering, He hath perfected for ever *them that are sanctified* whereof the Holy Spirit also is a witness to us." It might be proper to ask if God has no higher conception of "perfection" for His sin-hating, blood-bought and blood-washed children than that carnality should still remain in their hearts. And has the Holy Spirit no higher mission than to bear witness to every believer that he has within him an *"unremovable sin"* that is enmity against God?

Notice, further, that the noun "hagiasmos" derived from this adjective is used ten times in the New Testament. In the Revised Version it is always translated, "sanctification." It is used in the text, I. Thess. iv. 7, "For God hath not called you unto uncleanness but unto *sanctification:"* Now why is this sharp contrast made between *"uncleanness"* and *"sanctification,"* unless God, in sanctifying, removes the uncleanness of inbred sin entirely out of our being? If sanctification does not remove the indwelling sin, then the uncleanness still remains and the text becomes meaningless.

But inward repression of sin is not inward *purity* or *holiness* or *sanctification.* In justification and regeneration, as we have seen, depravity is held in subjugation, so that it does not rule the life. Therefore, if sanctification only represses depravity, it is not anything more than regeneration. But if that were true we cannot explain why all the regenerated are so constantly urged to be sanctified.

The inference is irresistible. Choking down or repressing sin, or counteracting it, is not the process of cleansing the heart. "Purge me, and I shall be clean; wash me, and I shall be whiter than snow." Repression is not purging, or washing. The inward impurities remaining in regeneration are removed by entire sanctification. "Holiness, or entire sanctification, is the carnal nature ERADICATED, DESTROYED, EXTERMINATED." Even as Jesus said, "Every tree that My Father hath not planted shall be ROOTED UP." He never planted carnality in human nature. The devil did it, and Christ will destroy the work of the devil, eradicate it from our hearts.

"The divine method of dealing with sin is always by extermination. All must see that the extirpation of inward pollution is Scriptural. Holiness is unmingled purity." The same noun is used in Heb. xii. 14: "Follow peace with all men, and THE SANCTIFICATION without which no man shall see the Lord." Now if the Pentecostal baptism with the Spirit that brings sanctification still leaves within us "the old man that is corrupt," "the evil heart of unbelief in departing from the living God," "the law of sin and death," "the carnal mind that is enmity against God," then in what conceivable sense does that unspeakable blessing fit us to *see God* and enjoy Him for ever?

This same wonderful adjective, "hagios," that has such a wealth of meaning, is used four times in that famous passage in I. Peter i. 15, 16: "Like as He Who called you is *holy,* be ye yourselves also *holy* in all manner of living, because it is written, Ye shall be *holy,* for I am *holy."* Here we are taught that our holiness, or sanctification, is to be "LIKE" God's. Could it be imagined that God and the angels are full of carnality and infested with propensity to sin? If not, why do some insist that the sanctifying baptism with the Holy Ghost still leaves us uncleansed from *"indwelling sin"?* May God open our eyes to see that God calls us to be *"cleansed," "sanctified,"* and have a holiness like His own. As Dr. Steele observes: "The repressive theory of holiness is out of harmony with Divine purity. Holiness in man must mean precisely the same as holiness in God, Who announces Himself as holy and then founds human obligation to holiness upon this revealed attribute. 'BE YE HOLY, for I AM HOLY.' Who dares to say that God's holiness is different in kind from man's holiness, save that one is original and the other is inwrought by the Holy Ghost?"

We come then to the same conclusion from this line of argument.

1. The adjective "hagios" means pure, righteous.
2. It is applied one hundred times to God.
3. We are commanded to have the spiritual quality denoted by this adjective LIKE AS God has it.

4. This adjective is the basis of the verb "*sanctify*" used sixteen times, and the noun, "hagiasmos," sanctification, used ten times, in reference to people.
5. The Holy Spirit does the sanctifying (Rom. xv. 16 and II. Thess. ii. 13).
6. The aorist tense shows that it is an instantaneous and completed action.
7. Acts xv. 8, 9 declares that this *cleansing,* or making holy, is produced by the Pentecostal baptism.

V. We believe that indwelling sin can be removed from the heart because of the doctrine of spiritual circumcision. Fifteen or twenty years after Abraham was justified he was called to be holy, had his name changed, and he was circumcised. The spiritual meaning of this was taught by Moses in Deut. xxx. 6: "And Jehovah thy God will circumcise thy heart and the heart of thy seed to love Jehovah thy God with all thy heart, and with all thy soul, that thou mayest live."

This spiritual meaning, the removal of *something* from the heart, was also taught by Jeremiah (Jer. iv. 4): "Circumcise yourselves to the Lord and TAKE AWAY the foreskin of your heart, ye men of Judah, and ye inhabitants of Jerusalem."

S. Paul endorsed that spiritual meaning when he wrote Rom. ii. 28, 29: "...Circumcision is that of the *heart,* in the spirit and not in the letter; whose praise is not of men but of God."

Undeniably something was removed from the physical being by circumcision. Jeremiah said that something was thus to be TAKEN AWAY (not suppressed) from the heart; and S. Paul reiterates the idea that something is to be removed from the heart by a *spiritual circumcision.* He explains what he means in Col. ii. 9-11: "In whom ye were also circumcised with a circumcision not made with hands in the putting off of the body of the flesh (sarx) in the circumcision of Christ." Bishop Ellicott says "the body of the flesh" in this passage is synonymous with "the body of sin" in Rom. vi. 6.

Dr. Steele, of Boston University, says: "We call the attention of every Greek scholar to the strength of the original noun "putting off." It is a word invented by Paul and found nowhere else in the Bible nor in the whole range of Greek literature. To show the thoroughness of the cleansing by the complete *stripping off* and *laying aside* of the propensity to evil, the apostle prefixes one preposition (apo) denoting separateness to another (ek) denoting outness (and joins to the stem of a verb denoting to strip or unclothe), and thus constructs the strongest conceivable term for the entire removal of depravity.

When I was a student at Yale, President Dwight declared that the commentator, Meyer, was the greatest New Testament exegete living. Professor Schaff, of New York, called him the prince of exegetes. This Meyer thus comments on the above passage, Col. ii, 9-I I, "Spiritual circumcision, divinely performed, consisted in a COMPLETE PARTING AND DOING AWAY WITH THIS BODY OF SIN, in so far as God, by means of this ethical circumcision, HAS TAKEN OFF AND REMOVED THE SINFUL BODY FROM MAN, LIKE A GARMENT DRAWN OFF AND LAID ASIDE."

And yet, in the face of God's own interpretation of this rite, and His plain declaration that God removes *the body of sin* (sarx), *"the old man"* of depravity from us in sanctification, and the testimony of the best Greek exegetes of the world as to the unmistakable meaning of the words, and the teaching of the passage, a Keswick speaker makes the astounding declaration that *"there is not a line of Scripture to support this position!"*

We would also ask another Keswick speaker if this teaching about spiritual circumcision warrants him in saying, "Every part of Scripture teaches the retention of corruption in man to the last hour of life." These assumptions are something amazing.

VI. We believe that indwelling sin can be removed from us because of what God says about purity and being pure. In Titus ii. 14 we are told that Jesus "gave Himself for us that He might PURIFY unto Himself a people for His own possession." Can Jesus do no better work of purifying in us than to leave us still infested with carnality and a spirit of alienation from God? Did the Son of God come from heaven to suffer death for a work so superficial and trivial? We cannot believe it for a moment.`

People who are already Christians are exhorted to "PURIFY their hearts" (hagnisate) (James iv. 8). The Bible says a great deal about being PURE and having PURITY. It must be a state of grace highly pleasing to God. He has set His heart upon sanctifying us so that we may have it.

Now this is one reason among others why we cannot accept the doctrine of suppression— it is not *purity.* The Bible has nothing to say concerning the suppression of indwelling sin, but rather its removal. It is not even hinted at in the blessed Book; but it does urge upon us *purity.*

Purity means freedom from defilement, unmixed, unpolluted. If anything is compounded with anything else it is adulterated and not pure. Water or air mixed with anything else is not pure; and the heart filled with depravity is not pure. A servant may sweep a room and not sweep under the mats: the dirt is left hidden and suppressed. It is a good example of *suppression,* but it is not PURITY. So sin held down and subdued, but still felt in the heart, is not purity. Hence suppression is only impurity. Some teachers tell us that this is the highest state of grace possible in this life, and they teach nothing more. But God pronounces no blessing upon it. Jesus says, "Blessed are the pure in heart, for they shall see God." This is in the present tense, therefore there must be people who have pure hearts and purity. To teach otherwise is to teach contrary to the Word of the Lord.

VII. We believe that our moral beings can be delivered from the pollution of depravity, because of what God has said about "*perfection*" and being "perfect."

The adjective "teleios" is used in the New Testament many times. It means "brought to completion," "fully accomplished," "fully realised," "without shortcoming," "perfect." It is used of persons ten times. Nouns and verbs derived from it and applied to persons are also used many times. We have such expressions as "Let us cleanse ourselves from all defilement of flesh and spirit, *perfecting holiness* in the fear of God" (II. Cor. vii. 1); "Wherefore, leaving the doctrine of the first principles of Christ, let us press on (or be borne on) unto *perfection*"; "Above all these things put on love, which is the bond of *perfectness*" (Col. iii. 14); "Let us therefore, as many as be *perfect,* be thus minded" (Phil. iii. 15); "Ye therefore shall be *perfect* as your Father in heaven is *perfect*" (Matt. v. 48).

The Holy Spirit surely meant something when He used this language, and these terms signify something that is precious to the heart of God. We believe that we can find some proper and definite meaning for these terms.

We get a valuable hint from I. Cor. iii. 1-3. Paul said the Corinthian Christians were *carnal* (sarkikoi)— even babes in Christ, and not spiritual (pneumatikoi). Then the "developed" Christians, the "*perfect*" Christians, would not be "carnal," "subject to the propensity of the flesh" (depravity, or pollution of the moral being). They would be sanctified or cleansed in their natures, and would be spiritual (pneumatikoi), having a nature derived from the Holy Spirit (Pneuma).

We believe this is what Christian perfection is. It is a cleansed, sanctified moral nature, obtained by the baptism with the Holy Ghost. It is a state of heart in which innate evil has been removed, and for it has been substituted perfect love to God and man.

Just here we hear objectors saying, "Perfectionist!"

"Perfectionism!" "Absolute perfection!!" "Sinless perfection!!" The Rev. E. W. Moore well says: "The phrase, 'sinless perfection,' is the devil's scarecrow to frighten God's people from the finest wheat. People are much more afraid of the doctrine of sinless perfection than they are of the practice of sinful imperfection."

Evangelical perfection, as revealed in the Bible, is not "absolute perfection." We never use that phrase, as God only has "absolute perfection." Our perfection is derived and inwrought by His grace.

Neither do we use the phrase, "sinless perfection." There was in the previous century a little obscure and short-lived company of people that claimed "sinless perfection." It generally means in its advocates a claim to *have never sinned,* or a claim that *they cannot sin,* both of which are unwarranted by the Bible. Accredited holiness teachers never use the phrase. Evangelical perfection is not "sinless perfection." "Sin, though forgiven," says Dr. Daniel Steele, "leaves scars and infirmities which look like sins to the prejudiced spectator. Hence Wesley refused to call the holiest saint on earth sinless, because the term would inevitably awaken a fruitless debate." Reader Harris wisely observed: "All intelligent believers are agreed that there is in this life no such experience as 'sinless perfection'; that is to say, a state in which the believer will not be tempted, will not be liable to fall, and will not need the abiding presence of Christ."

Rev. Harry Bisseker, M.A., writes judiciously on this subject, as follows:— "Our Lord's precept in Matt. v. 48 does not mean that our perfection is to equal the Father's perfection. (*a*) The word translated 'perfect' implies not *absolute* but *relative* perfection. Its strict signification is, 'brought to its proper end.' It is used to describe those who are *full-grown* in contrast with those who are babes (Eph. iv. 13, 14). So in character also, it is employed to denote those who have attained that *completeness which they were created to realise.* What it suggests, therefore, is only a perfection *relative to the end for which a person or thing exists.* The true sense of our Lord's words is given in the paraphrase, 'Ye in your sphere shall fully realise the end of your being, just as in His higher sphere your Father realises the end of His being.' He calls us to a life of purity and perfect love. He who has it has the perfection which Christ requires."

John Wesley's doctrine of perfection does not mean that our perfection was to equal the Father's perfection (in every sense).

(*a*) To the disciple as to his Lord, it is simply a doctrine of perfect love.

In a conference with clergymen Wesley was asked: "What is implied in being a perfect Christian?" "The loving God with all our heart and mind and soul," was the reply.

(*b*) This perfect love, he goes on to teach, does not yield a man *absolute* perfection. "He still grows in grace, in the knowledge of Christ, in the love and image of God; and will do so, not only till death but to all eternity.

(*c*) "Nor does it render its possessor immune from error. It does not imply, as some men seem to have imagined, an exemption either from ignorance, or mistake, or infirmities, or temptations." For this reason Wesley declined to use the term "sinless perfection."

(*d*) Nevertheless, he refused to treat such unintentional errors in a life of perfect love as though they were *sins.* "I believe a person filled with the love of God is still liable to involuntary transgressions. Such transgressions you may call sins if you please; I do not."

I am writing these pages within a few miles of a prominent preacher who ridicules Christian *perfection* and makes light of being *"filled with the Holy Ghost."* He does it openly before his congregation, and publicly declared: "We run the Christian race with the devil in our hearts and the malignity of sin in our lives." It is perfectly safe to affirm that this is not the Christian life that God holds up to us as our ideal. It is not the perfection that God demands of us, nor the kind of life He lovingly calls us to. To affirm that that is the best experience that we can have in this life is to insult the Omnipotent Christ and the Infinite Holy Spirit. If we will permit Him to do it, He Who cast the demons out of the Gadarene can cast the devil out of our hearts to-day, and the fiery baptism with the Holy Spirit will consume out of our beings the "malignity of sin." We can then realise "the end of our being" and the purpose for which we were created. God is pleased to call this "perfection." "Wherefore, leaving the doctrine of the first principles of Christ, let us press on unto perfection," thanking God for the privilege of walking with Him and serving Him with a holy, perfect heart.

As we have already seen in I. Cor. iii. 1, 2, carnality keeps Christians in abnormal babyhood and childhood. But in Eph. iv. 11-13 Paul tells us that "God gave apostles, prophets, evangelists, pastors, and teachers (and we may add, the Holy Spirit) for the *perfecting of the saints,* till we all attain to a *full-grown man,* unto the measure of the stature of the fulness of Christ, that we be no longer children."

Now, how can we reach this perfection unless the belittling, dwarfing "old man which is corrupt," is "put off," "crucified," "destroyed," "made dead," or "eliminated" out of our being? We are therefore forced to conclude either that God holds out to us a false hope of maturity and Christian perfection, or He has made ample provision for "taking away" from us the carnal mind. The former alternative is unthinkable; therefore we gladly accept the latter.

VIII. We are confirmed in our faith that God will remove inbred sin from us in this life by the teaching of the first chapter of the First Epistle of John. No passage of

Scripture has been worse misinterpreted or more industriously used to defend the unscriptural doctrine of necessary and continual sin.

Let the reader remember that an evil sect of false teachers had arisen, who held that all sin resided in the body, and taught that one could practise all enormities of vice and impurity, and still his soul would remain innocent and uninjured. The practices of these teachers soon became as bad as their doctrines, and they literally wallowed in profligacy. The apostle Peter wrote against them: "False teachers who shall privily bring in destructive heresies, denying even the Master that bought them. And many shall follow their lascivious doings: by reason of whom the way of truth shall be evil spoken of" (II. Peter ii. 1, 2). "Men that count it pleasure to revel in the day time, revelling in their deceivings while they feast with you. Having eyes full of adultery, and that cannot cease from sin; enticing unsteadfast souls: having a heart exercised in covetousness" (vv. 13 and 14).

Jude described them as "wild waves of the sea, foaming out their own shame... walking after their own lusts, and their mouth speaking great swelling words" (vv. 13-16).

When these vile teachers were urged by the holy apostles to repent, they replied that they did not need to repent. When urged to give up their vile sins, they replied that they had no sins and never had any. This awful delusion that sprang from heathen philosophy, akin to Christian Science of to-day, which also denies the existence of sin, was sweeping the churches from their moorings of faith.

When these false teachers were told that Jesus had a body and was holy, they then taught that Christ had only a phantom body, and therefore His atoning death was an unreality. This heresy, unless met vigorously, would wipe Christianity out of existence. So John wrote his First Epistle to meet this error and to give believers the true grounds of assurance. He says (I. John ii. 26), "These things have I written unto you concerning them that seduce you"; and iii. 7, "Little children, let no man deceive you."

Now, with this introduction concerning this heresy in mind, let us read the first chapter of John and a few verses in the second and third, and we shall be able to understand why the apostle wrote as he did and what he meant to teach. At the opening he says in substance: We know that Jesus was no phantom man, for we have *heard Him* with our ears, and *seen Him* with our eyes, and *handled Him* with our hands. We ate, and drank, and walked, and talked, and slept with Jesus for more than three years, and saw Him die on the Cross for our sins, and saw Him many times after He was risen, and we know that He was a real man and no phantom ghost.

Now, the next six verses, beginning with the fifth, are written in pairs; the first verse of each pair, viz., the 5th, 7th, and 9th verses, are the Christian truth of full salvation. But the contrasted— 6th, 8th, and 10th verses— are blows at the conduct and doctrine of the seducers of the churches. Notice them.

Verse 5. *Christian truth:* "God is light, and in Him is no darkness at all."

Verse 6. *A blow at the seducers:* "If we say that we have fellowship with Him, and walk in darkness (as these seducers say and do), we lie, and do not the truth."

Verse 7. *Christian truth about full salvation:* "But if we walk in the light as He is He that doeth sin are continually doing) is in the light, we have fellowship one with another, *and the blood of Jesus His Son cleanseth us from all sin."*

Verse 8. *Another blow at seducers:* "If we say that we have no sin (to be cleansed from, and no need of a Saviour, as these vile teachers are saying) we deceive ourselves, and the truth is not in us."

Verse 9. *Again the blessed truth of full salvation:* "If we confess our sins, He is faithful and righteous to forgive us our sins *and to cleanse us from all unrighteousness."*

Verse 10. *Another blow at seducers:* "If we say we have not sinned (as these seducers say) we make Him a liar, and His word is not in us."

Chapter ii., verse 4. *Other blows at seducers:* "He that saith I know Him, and keepeth not His commandments (as these drunken and licentious teachers are doing), is a liar, and the truth is not in him."

Verse 9. "He that saith he is in the light and hateth his brother is in darkness until now."

Chapter iii. 8. "He that doeth sin (as these seducers are continually doing) is of the devil."

This interpretation becomes very clear if we put the fifth, seventh and ninth verses together. They are in beautiful harmony, and teach in a wonderful way the doctrine of complete cleansing from all sin. Thus:

Verse 5. "God is light and in Him is no darkness at all."

Verse 7. "If we walk in the light as He is in the light we have fellowship one with another, *and the blood of Jesus His Son cleanseth us from all sin."*

Verse 9. "If we confess our sins He is faithful and righteous to forgive us our sins, *and to cleanse us from all unrighteousness."*

This is the Gibraltar of the Christian faith, the glorious gospel of *justification* and *sanctification.* Now it is perfectly safe to say that the inspired apostle was not referring to the same people in the eighth verse that he referred to in the seventh verse. It would be equivalent to saying, 7th verse, "If John Smith walks in the light as God is in the light, he has blessed holy fellowship with other saints, and the blood of Jesus, God's Son, cleanseth John Smith '*from all sin.*'" "But" (8th verse) "if John Smith should then bear testimony that he has no sin because his whole being has been cleansed *'from all sin,'* he deceives himself, and the truth is not in him!" Such an interpretation is manifestly absurd. Inspired apostles do not write such flat contradictions with the same penful of ink.

We conclude, therefore, that in the 6th, 8th and 10th verses he had in mind the seducers he was writing against, and here is the scathing arraignment of the error that was leading Church members to live in the deepest sin, and yet be so deluded by a heathenish doctrine that they could still profess to be walking in the light with God and declaring that they had no sin which needed the atoning blood. Read them together and mark the harmony.

6th verse. "If we say that we have fellowship with Him, and walk in darkness, we lie and do not the truth."

8th and 10th verses. "If we say we have no sin (to be cleansed from) ...and if we say we have not sinned (as these evil men are doing while practising vice themselves) we deceive ourselves, and make Him a liar, and the truth and His word are not in us."

Chapter ii. 4. "He that saith I know Him, and keepeth not His commandments, is a liar, and the truth is not in him."

This grouping of these passages makes the first chapter of I. John perfectly plain, and robs it of all its seeming contradictions. It is amazing that men, in the interests of teaching suppression and the doctrine of necessary and continual sin, should take the words of the eighth verse, intended as a warning to wicked deceivers, and apply them to the holy children of God professing sanctification. It is doubtful if men ever made a greater perversion and misapplication of Scripture.

Listen to some great scholars on the subject. Bishop Westcott, commenting on verse 7, "Cleanseth from all sin," says: "The thought here is of sin, and not of sins; of the spring, the principle, and not of the separate manifestations." In other words, he affirms that the blood of Christ cleanses from the "principle of sin."

Dean Alford says on verse 9: "Observe the two verbs (forgive, cleanse) are aorist, because the purpose of the faithfulness and justice of God is to do each, to justify and to sanctify wholly and entirely." This is exactly what we are contending for, namely, that the Holy Spirit in sanctifying *cleanses* us "from all unrighteousness" (unrightness).

Adam Clarke says on this whole passage: "Sin exists in the soul after two modes or forms: (1) In *guilt,* which requires forgiveness or pardon; (2) in *pollution,* which requires *cleansing...* As 'all unrighteousness is sin,' so he that is cleansed from all unrighteousness is cleansed from all sin. To attempt to evade this, and *plead for the continuance of sin in the heart through life, is ungrateful, wicked, and even blasphemous;* for as he who says he has not sinned, makes God a liar, Who has declared to the contrary, so he that says *the blood of Christ* either *cannot or will not cleanse us from all sin in this life,* GIVES ALSO THE LIE TO HIS MAKER, Who has declared to the contrary, and he thus shows that the Word— the doctrine of God— is not in him. Reader, it is the birthright of every child of God to be CLEANSED FROM ALL SIN, to keep himself unspotted from the world, and so to live as nevermore to offend his Maker."

IX. We are driven to our conclusion that the sanctifying work of the Holy Spirit actually cleanses the whole being from indwelling sin, by the teaching of the *third* chapter of I. John. It harmonises perfectly with the first chapter. They both sing the same message of holiness in the same *heart-cleansing from all sin.*

Verse 3: "And every one that hath this hope set on Him (Jesus) purifieth (hagnizei) himself even as (kathos) He (Christ) is pure (hagnos)." The definitions of the adjective hagnos are "pure, chaste, modest, innocent, blameless." The noun derived from it means, "a life of purity." The verb derived from it means, "to purify morally." Fortunately we are not left in doubt as to what extent this purifying in a believer's heart may be carried on. He purifies himself, by the help of God, "EVEN AS CHRIST HIS LORD IS PURE."

A book lies before me written by a man well known in the Christian world. In it I find this passage: "The holiest believer must each moment confess that *he has sin within him*— the flesh, namely, in which dwelleth no good thing." ... "I have read of a young lion whom nothing could awe or keep down but the eye of his keeper." With the keeper you could come near him, and he would crouch, his savage nature all unchanged, and thirsting for blood, trembling at the keeper's feet. You might put your foot on his neck, as long as the keeper was with you. To approach him without the keeper would be instant death. And so it is that the believer can *have sin* and yet not *do sin.* The *evil nature* is unchanged in its enmity against God, but the abiding presence of Jesus keeps it down. In faith the believer entrusts himself to the keeping, to the indwelling of the Son of God; he abides in Him, and counts on Jesus to abide in him too. The union and fellowship is the secret of a holy life. 'In Him is no sin; he that abideth in Him sinneth not.'"

Now, how does this tally with the inspired assertion, "The blood of Jesus His Son CLEANSETH US FROM ALL SIN"? How does it measure up to the assertion, "Every one that hath this hope set on Him (Christ) purifieth himself EVEN AS (kathos) He (Jesus) is pure"? It is in utter disagreement with the Word of God. Just as Jesus had no carnality, neither need we have such a thing in us.

Let us now go on with our third chapter of I. John. 3rd verse: We are to be pure, "even as," "according as," "just as," Christ is pure. Adam Clark makes this appropriate comment: "The words may be understood of a man anxiously using all the means that lead to purity; and imploring God for the sanctifying Spirit to cleanse the thoughts of his heart till he is as completely saved from his sins as Christ was free from sin."

Many tell us that "this never can be done, for no man can be saved from sin in this life." Or, as another says: "The holiest believer must each moment confess that HE HAS SIN WITHIN HIM." ... "The deepest consciousness of having still an evil and corrupt nature in the present, may consist with humble but joyful praise to Him Who keeps from stumbling."

We would ask those who teach the suppression of sin, How much sin may we be saved from in this life? Something ought to be ascertained on this subject: (1) That the soul may have some *determinate object* in view; (2) That it may not lose its time in praying for what is impossible of attainment. Now as He was manifested to take away our sins (verse 5), to destroy the works of the devil (verse 8), and as His blood cleanseth us from all sin and unrighteousness (ch. i. 7 and 9), is it not evident that God means that believers in Christ shall be saved from ALL SIN? May not the "holiest believer" have a better state of heart than one still defiled with sin? Is such a heart "cleansed from ALL SIN"?

How can men, in the face of such Scriptures, still dare to maintain that no man can be saved from indwelling sin in this life?

Adam Clark observes: "It is a miserable salvo for Christians to say that they do not sin as much as they used to; and they do not sin habitually, only occasionally. Alas! for this system! Could not the grace that saved them *partially,* save them *perfectly?* Could not that power of God that saved them from *habitual* sin, save them from *occasional* sin? Shall we suppose that sin, how potent soever it may be, is as potent as the Spirit and grace of Christ? And if it were for God's glory and their good that they were *partially saved,* would it not have been *more* for God's glory and their good if they had been PERFECTLY saved?"

Verse 5: "And ye know that He was manifested to take away sins; and in Him is no sin." "Christ came into the world to destroy the power, pardon the guilt, and CLEANSE FROM THE POLLUTION OF SIN. This was the very design of His manifestation in the flesh. He was born, suffered and died for this very purpose; and can it be supposed that He either CAN NOT or WILL NOT accomplish the object of His coming?

Verse 8: "To this end was the Son of God manifested that He might destroy the works of the devil." The greatest work of the devil was to inject depravity into the race at its fountain, to be propagated by race connection, and repeated in every child born into the world. But Jesus was manifested with this very design, that He might destroy (luo), THAT HE MIGHT LOOSE the bonds of sin, and dissolve its power, influence and connexion with us.

The completeness of Jesus' work in delivering us from the work of the devil is shown by the meanings of the verb used: they are "to loosen," "to unbind," "to disengage," "set free," "deliver," "break up," "destroy," "demolish." What a glorious deliverance we may have from Jesus! But a Keswick speaker belittles this by the following comment on this passage: "It is no doubt true that Christ is going to destroy the works of the devil. But there is nothing in those words to show that He does so in our hearts, either *immediately* or *suddenly.* We must infer that the process of destruction is a *gradual* one, wrought in successive stages." We will answer through Bishop Westcott and Dean Alford.

Bishop Westcott says: "The two objects of the manifestation of Christ cover the whole work of redemption: 'to take away sins' (verse 5), and 'to destroy the works of the devil' (verse 8). In this connection the works of the devil are gathered up in 'sin' (indwelling sin), which is their spring. This the devil has wrought in men. The efficacy of Christ's work extends both to 'sins' and to 'sin.'"

Dean Alford points out that the aorist tense for the verbs 'take away' and 'destroy' implies "TAKE AWAY AT ONE ACT AND ENTIRELY."

Dr. Daniel Steele, in his noble essay on "The tense readings of the Greek Testament," says of the aorist tense in Rom. vi. 6: "The aorist here teaches the possibility of an instantaneous death-stroke to inbred sin, and that there is no need of a slow and painful process, lingering till physical death or purgatorial fire ends the torment." He says in closing: "We have looked in vain for one of the verbs denoting sanctification or perfection in the imperfect tense (which would teach a progressive work). The verb *hagiazo,* "to sanctify," is always aorist or perfect. The same may be said of the verbs katharizo, "to cleanse," and hagnizo, "to purify." Our inference is that the energy of the Holy Spirit in the work of entire sanctification, however long the preparation, IS PUT FORTH AT A STROKE BY A MOMENTARY ACT."

This is corroborated by the universal testimony of those who have experienced this grace.

The truth is, we have the most critical and scholarly commentaries and Greek exegetes, the lexicons and grammars, on our side in this matter. If the Greek New Testament can teach anything by nouns, adjectives and verbs, and even adverbs and prepositions, about a spiritual experience, our doctrine of sanctification, as a heart-cleansing work, is taught by the Word of God. "Repressive power is nowhere ascribed to the blood of Christ, but rather purgative efficacy." And its sanctifying work is immediate in the life.

X. We are strengthened in our faith that carnality can be removed through the baptism with the Holy Spirit, by the very meaning of "BAPTISM." It signifies CLEANSING. Its symbols are water and fire, and these are the elements used. They are the two things used in cleansing in this world. Water cleanses the *outside;* fire cleanses the very material of which a thing is composed.

Dr. Daniel Steele wrote: "In trying to show that entire sanctification is nowhere connected with the Spirit-baptism, a Keswick speaker fails in his explanation of 'fire' in the phrase 'baptism with the Holy Ghost and fire,' to note that fire is A PURIFYING ELEMENT, and is here associated with the Spirit by the rhetorical figure of '*hendiadys*' (one idea expressed by two nouns). Since earthen and metallic vessels cannot be perfectly cleansed by *water, fire* is employed as the most perfect purifier. Water symbolizes the initial cleansing, and fire symbolises the complete purification wrought by the Holy Spirit in Pentecostal fulness."

A Keswick preacher's sermon in print lies before me. It was preached in London. In it he said: "The second thing that fire does is to purify. In Mal. iii. 1-3 we are told of the purifying power of fire. There is nothing that purifies like fire. Water does not cleanse like fire, Suppose I have a piece of gold and there is filth on the outside of it, how can I get it off? I can wash it off with water. But suppose the dirt is inside it, how will I get it out? There is but one way— throw it into the fire. And, men and women, if the filth is on the outside with us, it can be washed away by the water of the Word; but the trouble is that the filth is on the inside; and what we need is the fire of the Holy Ghost, penetrating to the innermost depths of our being—burning, burning! cleansing, cleansing, cleansing!

What a refining came to the apostles on that day of Pentecost! How full of self-seeking they had been, up to the very last supper! At that last supper they had a dispute as to who should be first in the Kingdom (Luke xxii. 24), but after Pentecost that was all gone. It was no longer self, but Christ. How weak and cowardly they had been right up to the crucifixion! They all forsook Him and fled; and Peter denied Him at the accusation of a servant maid, with oaths and curses; but after Pentecost that was all gone. There was no more of that. That same Peter who had cursed and sworn and denied, faced the very Council that had condemned Jesus to death, and said to them "Ye rulers of the people and elders of Israel, if we this day be examined of the good deed done to the impotent man, by what means he is made whole, be it known unto you, and to all the people of Israel, that by the name of Jesus Christ of Nazareth, Whom ye crucified, Whom God raised from the dead, even by Him doth this man stand before you whole." Oh! friends, cleansing is a very slow process by ordinary methods, but A BAPTISM OF FIRE DOES MARVELS IN A MOMENT!

In the third place the Bible teaches us that fire consumes. In Ezekiel xxiv. 11-13 we are told of the consuming power of fire, the power of judgment which is there consuming the filth and dross of Jerusalem; and the baptism of fire consumes and cleanses *all* PRIDE, *all* VANITY, all SELFISHNESS, all PERSONAL AMBITION, all UNGOVERNABLE TEMPER.

Oh! isn't that what we Christians need— a fire that will burn up all that SELF-SEEKING, and PRIDE, and WORLDLINESS of ours which is hindering the world from coming to Christ? You women, who have unconverted husbands, isn't that what you need?— a baptism of fire that will transform your life, so that your husbands will say, "I must have what my wife has got."

Now that is exactly what the regular preachers of holiness are teaching, year in and year out, namely, the fiery baptism with the Holy Ghost for heart-cleansing and sanctification. But this same Keswick speaker published this statement in one of his books: "*There is a line of teaching on this subject that leads men to expect that if they receive the baptism with the Holy Spirit, the old carnal nature will be eradicated.* THERE IS NOT A LINE OF SCRIPTURE TO SUPPORT THIS POSITION."

Now, someone may ask, How could this man preach such a straight, ringing sermon on the PURIFYING, HEART-CLEANSING FIRE OF THE HOLY-GHOST BAPTISM and flatly deny it in a book? To use [*sic*] the answer is plain. He was preaching under the unction of the Holy Spirit, and he preached the truth. He was writing a book in cold blood without the heavenly unction, and he taught the Holy Ghost for *power* but not for *cleansing.* Certainly the Holy Spirit never inspired him to contradict the Word of God. Peter said to the Council in Jerusalem, as recorded in Acts xv. 8, 9, "*And God, Who knoweth the heart, bare them witness, giving them the Holy Ghost, even as He did unto us: and He made no distinction between us and them,* CLEANSING THEIR HEARTS BY FAITH." Now, here is a declaration, as plain as language could well make it, that the baptism with the Holy Ghost, the Pentecostal blessing, cleansed the Jewish apostles and disciples, and also cleansed the hearts of the Gentiles, and that GOD BORE WITNESS TO THE CLEANSING. The speaker referred to exactly teaches this in a sermon, and exactly contradicts it in a book. How can he thus contradict himself, unless he does so to defend a theory.

But someone may reply, Perhaps the whole being—body, soul and spirit— are not cleansed by the sanctifying baptism. We reply, Yes, they are, for Paul prays (I. Thess. v. 23), "And the God of peace Himself sanctify you wholly (holoteleis, 'wholly,' 'to the end,' 'quite completely,' 'through and through'), and may your SPIRIT and SOUL and BODY be preserved entire." A man is to be sanctified, *spirit, soul and body,* and kept so.

Another passage bears us out in this interpretation, namely, II. Cor. vii. 1: "Having, therefore, these promises, beloved, let us cleanse ourselves from all DEFILEMENT OF FLESH AND SPIRIT, perfecting holiness in the fear of God." Not even the body is to remain a hiding-place for old carnality. It is to be "a temple of the living God"; even as God said, "I will dwell in them and walk in them; and I will be their God, and they shall be My people."

Just here, another person may ask, Why all this discussion? Is it not just as well to have carnality *suppressed in us* as to have it *removed from us?* We might answer in many ways. It is better to have a PURE heart than to have an IMPURE heart. It is better to be *like* God than to be *unlike* Him. It is better to *please* than to *dis*please God. He has set His heart on CLEANSING US FROM ALL SIN. For that end He gave His Son to die. We ought to *want* what Jesus died for.

Moreover, indwelling sin is dangerous. It taxes our spiritual strength and resources to guard against it. It is like dynamite stored in the cellar. It may go off and blow every fair and holy thing in the soul to atoms. John Fletcher said: "So much of indwelling sin as we carry about with us, is so much of indwelling hell; so much of the sting which pierces the damned, so much of the spiritual fire which will burn up the wicked, so much of the never-dying worm which will prey upon them, so much of the dreadful instruments that will rack them, so much of Satan's image that will frighten them, so much of the characteristic by which the devil's children will be distinguished from the children of God, so much of the black mark by which the goats will be distinguished from the sheep.

To plead, therefore, for the continuance of indwelling sin is no better than to plead for keeping within your hearts one of the sharpest stings of death and one of the hottest coals in hell fire. On the other hand, to obtain Christian perfection is to have the last feature of Belial's image erased from your loving souls, the last bit of sting of death extracted from your composed breasts, and the last spark of hell fire extinguished in your peaceful bosoms."

We all need such a salvation as we have been describing. Forms of sin, attractive to the carnal mind, abound on every hand. We need to be made dead to their insidious charms. Every thing that is inflammatory, and can be kindled by the sparks of hell, should be removed from our beings.

This is an age of magnets and dynamos. The watches of men in our great cities get affected and untrue, and accidents occur on every side. In the eastern part of the United States the strongest magnet in the world was made. Two cannons fourteen feet long, were wound with eight miles of wire about each, and electricity turned on. So great was its magnetic power that ordinary watches were stopped in men's pockets eight feet away. But one manufacturer made a watch that could be held within six inches and the second hand not be affected a tick, as was testified by a dozen experts. The watch was absolutely DEMAGNETISED. Now, that is just what every Christian in the world needs. We must have a DEMAGNETISED, UNWORLDED BEING. We need a salvation that will make us dead to sin in every form. That is just the full salvation which Jesus has provided, and which we are offering to a sin-sick world.

Chapter IV.
Getting the Blessing, Growing in It, and Keeping It.

If there really is such a blessing of full salvation, as has been described in the preceding pages, it is important to know how it is to be obtained. We answer first negatively.

(1) We cannot get it by *pardon.* We did not get our depravity, or indwelling sin, through any fault of ours. We were born with it, just as we were born with a head on the top of our spinal column. We were no more responsible for one fact than for the other. So it is not pardoned away from us, and is not obtained with the first blessing of pardon.

(2) We cannot get it by *self-development or culture.* Human efforts at self-reformation, and tears, and struggles for self-betterment will never avail. Education and intellectual training, College diplomas and University degrees, will all fail of success.

(3) We cannot get it by *growth.* Like justification, sanctification is a work of God. No one can grow into a work of God. No sound religious teacher would tell a sinner to

grow into justification. It is a judicial act of God that sets aside the penalty of sin and brings pardon to the guilty soul. It is done in an instant. So is sanctification a definite, gracious *work of the Spirit of God wrought in us instantaneously* whereby the *believer is freed from sin,* and exalted to *holiness of heart and life.* The aorist tenses used in the prayers and exhortations and assertions about sanctification in the New Testament prove that we are sanctified *at once "by a momentary act" of the Holy Spirit.* The lexicons tell us (as we have shown in chapter I.) that we are sanctified by an "act of God," and God is not thirty or forty years putting forth an act. This rules out all slow processes, and the "get-it-by-growth" theory. This is true in philosophy and in experience. After we obtain the grace of sanctification as a gift from God, we can grow *in* it; but we cannot grow *into* it. It is received by faith *instantaneously,* through the baptism with the Holy Spirit.

It becomes important, then, to know how to obtain this blessing. In my book "Holiness and Power," the conditions of receiving the blessing are set forth with great care and fulness, with many illustrations. Here are the main conditions:

(1) A sense of the *need of the blessing;* a deep conviction of want. "Blessed are the poor in spirit, for theirs is the kingdom of heaven." Blessed are the souls who are not satisfied to have a low type of piety, and to live continually in the very lowest state of grace that they dare to think will keep them out of hell. Blessed are the Christians who are not at ease in an up-and-down, in-and out experience, mostly down and out, who are not content to let the "old man" of sin dwell within them, making unremitting warfare upon everything Christ-like in the heart. Blessed are the believers who will not rest while the carnal mind is within them—the inveterate foe of Jesus their Lord. Yea, thrice blessed are the justified souls, who do not indolently say: "I

am rich and increased with goods, and have need of nothing." The conviction of soul-poverty and a sense of need is a prophecy of good things to come.

(2) An assurance that *the blessing is for you.* None will seek this great experience if they think it is only for apostles and prophets and great dignitaries of the Churches, and a few evangelists like Wesley, Whitefield, and Finney. "The promise is unto you and to your children and to all that are afar off, even to as many as the Lord our God shall call." Every one that is called to be a Christian at all, is called to be a sanctified Christian, filled with the Holy Spirit, and endued with power for service. "This is the will of God, even your sanctification… for God hath called you… unto sanctification" (I. Thess. iv. 3 and 7). Write your own name in the assurance and call, and make them yours.

(3) "Blessed are they that *hunger and thirst* after righteousness, for they shall be filled." A deep craving for deliverance from indwelling sin; a heart-hunger to be more and more like Jesus, the Pattern and Ideal of holiness; a thirst for *God* and His character inwrought in us, as the hart pants after the water-brooks; a deathless desire to be rid of sin, and to be holy in life because pure in heart. This, oh this, is one of the great conditions of getting the blessing! When one feels as if he would die if he did not get the blessing, and almost would rather die than be without it, then Jesus will be getting ready to baptise with the Holy Spirit. He is looking round for candidates for the baptism. He will not fail to recognise the hearts that are crying out for holiness.

(4) Another condition for the blessing is *prayer.* "Our heavenly Father gives the Holy Spirit to them that *ask* Him." If the first three conditions are fully complied with, the deep cravings of the heart will find expression in prayer. Night and day the incense of petition will rise to God. There will be an importunity of supplication which

will take no denial. A hungry child will call on its parent for bread. A spiritual child, with a heart craving righteousness, will resort to prayer, the instinctive language of the soul. Prayer is a thing of Divine appointment, a privilege granted by God. A heart that is drawing nigh to God will certainly make use of its privilege and let its wants be known.

(5) Another condition of getting the blessing will be the spirit of *complete obedience,* an *absolutely surrendered soul.* All sin has in it the element of hostility and alienation from God. "The carnal mind is enmity against God; for it is not subject to the law of God, neither indeed can be" (Rom. viii. 7). Whoever would be rid of this internal spirit of alienation, "this evil heart of unbelief in departing from the living God," must surrender unreservedly to the sweet and blessed will of God. "God hath given *the Holy Spirit to them that obey Him*" (Acts v. 32).

This is one unalterable condition of receiving a clean heart. The Holy Spirit cannot be poured out upon us, while there is a shadow of rebellion in us to the Divine will. We must consent *to do, to be, to say, to go, to endure, to surrender, to suffer* as God wills. It would be absolutely unsafe and wrong to make any such surrender of self to any finite being in the universe. They might make unwise and unjust and harmful claims upon us with which we could not properly comply. But our God is infinitely wise and infinitely good, too wise to make a mistake and too good to be unkind. What He asks of us is the best for us; and there is no safe place in the universe for any of us but in the centre of His blessed will.

(6) Another condition of receiving the blessing is *complete consecration. "Yield* yourselves unto God, as those that are alive from the dead, and your members as instruments of righteousness unto God" (Rom. vi. 13). "I beseech you therefore, brethren, by the mercies of God, *to present* your bodies a living sacrifice, holy and accept-

able to God, which is your reasonable service" (Rom. xii. 1). The verbs for "yield" and "present" are the same in the Greek, and in both passages are in the aorist tense, teaching a *complete act, done once for all.*

Whoever would receive the baptism with the Holy Spirit for a clean heart, must turn himself over into God's hands for God to own and control for ever. Never once think again that you are your own. When the sinner comes to the altar to receive pardon, by sincere *repentance* he gives up *his bad things;* but when a Christian comes to the altar seeking the baptism with the Holy Spirit, he gives up to God all *his good things.* He avows God's ownership over him, and God's absolute right to him for ever, as having created him for His glory, and preserved him by His providence, and bought him with His blood.

Bring, then, yourself, your all, to God. Bring your body to be the temple of the Holy Ghost, to be kept from evil habits, and to be fed and cared for and clothed for God. Bring your eyes to see for God, and your ears to hear for God, and your lips to speak for God, and your hands to toil for God, and your feet to walk only in paths of righteousness where Jesus would walk. Bring your mind to think for God, and your will to choose for God, and to evermore ratify His blessed will. Bring your whole being to be the throne and kingdom of Jesus, for Him to inhabit and rule over and control. Bring your time to be used for God's glory, and your influence to be exerted for Him, and your reputation to be kept by Him, and to be trampled upon, if need be, because you walk with God (see Heb. xi. 32-40). Bring your family, your friends, your possessions. Bring out your Isaac, your very son Isaac, the thing that is dearest to your heart, and put him on the altar, and get on it yourself. Jesus is the altar (Heb. xiii. 10-12). Turn over everything to Him for your cleansing. God takes everybody for His possession that He can get, and He cleanses all who permit it by the fiery purifying of the Holy Spirit.

(7) The last condition of receiving the blessing is *faith.* We receive the Spirit by faith (Gal. iii. 3). Our hearts are "cleansed by faith" (Acts xv. 9). Now, when every particle of opposition to the will of God is gone, and the heart hungers for holiness, and pleads for the cleansing baptism by earnest prayer, and when one is willing to pay the price of dying out to the world and sin, and letting God have absolute ownership, and when everything is thus actually turned over to Him, the child of God has come to believing ground. He then *can believe* and *has a right to believe* the promise: "Faithful is He that calleth you (to sanctification), Who also will do it" (I. Thess. iv. 7 and v. 24). He has a right to believe that, as he has responded to the call of God and complied with the conditions announced by God, He then and there does baptise with the Holy Spirit, and the work is done.

Without any feeling or internal evidence, one must step out on the naked promise of God and believe that the work is done, because of God's assurance. The witness comes afterwards. Just as the sin-sick sinner repents and believes for pardon and receives the witness afterwards, so must the believing heart for sanctification. The order cannot be reversed. It is of Divine appointment that we believe first, and *feel* the joy and gladness afterward. Sometimes the witness must be waited for; we must look up and abide in faith, and wait. "Ye have need of patience, that after ye have done the will of God ye might receive the promise" (Heb. x. 35-38).

On Growth in Grace

A clean heart or Christian perfection does not exclude growth in grace. The pure in heart grow faster than any others. There is no state of grace which excludes progression. There is no standing still in a Christian life. "It is like riding a bicycle: you must go forward or fall." One must "progress or retrogress." If we are walking in the light and keeping up to it, we are growing. If refusing to do it, and neglecting present privilege and duty, we are backsliding, whatever our attainments may have been.

But, asks one, how can holiness be perfect and yet progressive? A most thoughtful teacher, the Rev. J. A. Wood, answers: "Perfection in quality does not exclude increase in quantity. Beyond entire sanctification there is no increase in purity, as that which is pure cannot be more than pure; but there may be unlimited increase in expansion and quantity. After love is made perfect, it may abound more and more. The capacities of the soul are expansive and progressive, and holiness in measure may increase, corresponding to increasing capacity. Faith, love, humility and patience may be perfect in kind and yet increase in volume and power. A tree may be perfectly sound, healthy, and vigorous in its branches, leaves and fruit, and yet year by year increase in capacity and fruitfulness."

Analogous to this is a wicked life. The Church has always held the doctrine of total depravity, and yet believed in the possibility of increasing depravity.

Someone may ask how a sanctified soul can grow more rapidly than others. The reasons are plain. Holiness does not put a finality to anything but the practice and dominion of sin. The soul full of love, and free from a proclivity to evil, and filled with the Spirit, is in the best possible condition to grow. The internal antagonisms to growth in grace are all removed. The removal of all weeds from the garden sends all the strength and moisture of the soil to the plants. The weeds of carnality are the greatest obstacles to the growth of Christian graces in the heart. When they are removed the graces thrive.

Then, too, the purified heart has stronger faith, clearer light, more uninterrupted communion with God, and dwells in a purer spiritual atmosphere than it did before it was cleansed. Moreover, the death of sin gives full scope to the life of righteousness. The very conditions of retaining purity are precisely those which are most conducive to growth in the knowledge of God and likeness to Christ.

Purity as Distinguished from Maturity.

The command of God to every Christian is, "Be filled with the Spirit." Many suppose this is only for mature Christians, and they put off obedience into the distant future and hope to grow into it. This is a serious mistake. We must not fail to distinguish between *purity* and *maturity.* It requires time and the slow process of development to reach maturity. Indeed, that is only a variable term; for we shall grow for ever in likeness to God. The Lord, through the baptism with the Holy Spirit, can make a new convert of a few days or weeks of experience as pure and clean as an experienced Christian. He can fill the soul of a new convert as completely as the soul of a Christian who has been a long time in the way. A thimble can be as full of ocean water as a vast sunken steamer. Each may be full to the measure of its capacity. So a young believer may be entirely consecrated, thoroughly cleansed, and blessedly filled with the Spirit as well as an aged believer. An oak tree only ten feet high is as purely oak in its nature as it will be when it is one hundred feet high; but it is not as mature.

God does not expect new converts to become mature Christians at once, but He does expect them to be filled with the Spirit and be cleansed, and like Him. Maturity is not a condition of gaining heaven, but sanctification is. "Without the sanctification no man shall see the Lord" (Heb, xii. 14). That preparation God wants us to have now. Jesus prayed for it (John xvii. 17) and died for it (Heb. xiii. 12), and declares that it is His will (I. Thess. iv. 3). and He calls us to it (I. Thess. iv. 7). and promises it (I.

Thess. v. 24). That blessing each true Christian may have now. Seek it, then, by faith, and receive it now as a blessing bought by the blood of Christ and promised to every believer now.

We can be Kept in this Blessing.

Some hold back from claiming this blessing lest they should not be able to keep it. This is a species of unbelief and a reflection on God's power and goodness. If He calls us to sanctification, and delights in holiness, is it not likely that He knows all our needs and has made full provision for our complete and abiding salvation?

Let us listen to His promises and trust His word. "My God shall supply every need of yours according to His riches in glory" (Phil. iv. 19). "He is able to keep you from stumbling" (Jude 24). "He is able to build you up and to give you an inheritance among all them that are sanctified" (Acts xx. 32). He is able to sanctify you wholly and to preserve you, spirit, soul and body, blameless (I. Thess. v. 23). "According as His Divine power hath given unto us all things that pertain unto life and godliness." "Who hath blessed us with all spiritual blessings." "And He is able to make all grace abound toward you that ye always, having all-sufficiency in all things, may abound to every good work" (II. Cor. ix. 8).

Chapter V.
This Kind of a Blessing is the Longing of Devout Souls.

I TURN TO "The Book of Common Prayer" of the Church of England, and read:

1. "Grant that we may hereafter live a *godly, righteous and sober life.*" ...
2. "And that the rest of our life hereafter may be *pure* and *holy.*"
3. "Vouchsafe, O Lord, to keep us this day *without sin.*"
4. "O God, *make clean our hearts* within us."
5. "Grant that this day we may *fall into no sin.*"
6. "Grant that... we may evermore serve Thee in *holiness and pureness* of living."
7. "And that we may show forth Thy praise... by walking before Thee in *holiness* and *righteousness* all our days."
8. "O God. Whose blessed Son was manifested that He might destroy the works of the devil, and make us the sons of God and heirs of eternal life; grant us, we beseech Thee, that, having this hope, we may *purify ourselves, even as He is pure.*"

9. "Keep us... *from all evil thoughts* which may assault and hurt the soul."
10. "*Cleanse* the thoughts of our hearts by the inspiration of Thy Holy Spirit, that we may perfectly love Thee."
11. "Give grace, that they may... truly serve Thee in *holiness and righteousness all the days of their life."*
12. "Submitting ourselves wholly to His holy will, and studying to serve Him in true *holiness and righteousness all the days of our life."*
13. "Grant that our sinful *bodies* may be *made clean* by His body, and our *souls washed* through His most precious blood."
14. "And here we offer and present unto Thee, O Lord, ourselves, our souls and bodies, to be a *reasonable, holy and living sacrifice* unto Thee."
15. "O Almighty Lord, we beseech Thee ... to direct, *sanctify and govern, both our hearts and bodies."*
16. "Humbly we beseech Thee to grant that we being *dead unto sin* and *living* unto *righteousness,* and being buried with Christ in His death, *may crucify the old man* and UTTERLY ABOLISH THE WHOLE BODY OF SIN."
17. "And that He will keep us *from all sin."*

There are many more passages of similar import that might be cited. But these are sufficient to show that our teaching is in harmony with the supplications and longings of devout hearts, as expressed in the Book of Common Prayer.

Wesley and Methodism.

John Wesley correctly interpreted the real inner spirit of the Church of England, of which he was a member. Rev. John S. Banks, in his "Theology," p. 222, says: "Methodism has always made the *destruction of inbred sin* part, and the chief part, of perfect holiness. At the same time this is kept in the closest connection with the atonement as the power, and faith as the condition: and who will set limits to either the one or the other? We believe that Methodism has not gone beyond the highest aspirations of the best Christians in all ages, either in its account of the blessing or in the prominence given to it. On this subject the saints of all Churches are in advance of theologians, and better represent the mind of Scripture. Methodism simply puts their faith and experience into formal statement, and gives it due prominence. To do this is part of its mission."

Bishop J. S. Key wrote on Holiness as a Methodist doctrine: "I affirm to-day, with all possible emphasis, that *salvation from all sin, received now by simple faith,* is the distinguishing doctrine of Methodism, which differentiates it from all other Churches. Leave this out and your Church is indefensible… Let me re-affirm. Your Church is for holiness or for nothing. Take that out of your preaching and it is emasculated. Take it out of your living, and you have nothing left worth your time and effort. Outside of heart-purity received and enjoyed now, you hold to no tenet that is not held and taught by some other Church, and in many instances can be better urged by them. *To raise up a holy people is our peculiar and exclusive mission.* This conviction seems to have been inwrought into the thought and conscience of our leaders from the beginning…

"Here, then, is our defence. We preach heart-purity and Christian perfection, because for this purpose God has raised us up, and on this mission has He sent us forth. *Silence would be sin…* In other words, if God called Methodism into being for the single purpose of *preaching and practising holiness,* we must do that at the peril of His displeasure and abandonment. We have no latitude of choice. We are shut up to our one mission. *We must fulfil the purpose of our being or pass away.* Other Churches may live and prosper with different inspirations, because raised for different ends, but Methodism must be childlike and consecrated and pure, or die.

"If the Methodist Church fails to accomplish her given work in her own appointed way, and begins to catch the spirit of the world and formal Churches around her, *her mission is at an end, and God will raise up some other to take her place and do her work.* The history of the past has demonstrated that *God can easier raise up a new Church than revive a dead one."*

The Salvation Army.

The Salvation Army, while Mrs. Booth was alive, was very strong on the teaching and experience of full salvation from all sin, and held to the doctrine we have set forth. A single quotation from their writings will show this: "We believe that after conversion there remains in the heart of the believer *inclinations to evil, or roots of bitterness,* which, unless overpowered by divine grace, produce actual sin: but that *these evil tendencies can be entirely taken away by the Spirit of God."*

The National Holiness Association of U.S.A.

This Association was organised some forty years ago to supplement the work of the Church in spreading holiness. It holds conventions in winter, and camp-meetings in summer. Rev. C. J. Fowler, D.D., is President. It probably has one hundred ministers elected to its body, and back of them there are not less than four hundred other ministers preaching the doctrine of Scriptural holiness as we have set it forth. The author himself is a member of the National Holiness Association.

There are not less than four hundred annual camp-meetings held in the United States that are convened solely for the spread of holiness. There are now ten weekly holiness papers that have each a weekly circulation of from 5,000 to 50,000. There are ten colleges planted to educate young people, and especially ministers, to spread holiness, as we are teaching it.

[The Free Methodist Church and The Pentecostal Church of the Nazarene]

The Free Methodist Church, from its origin, has been a Holiness Church; and The Pentecostal Church of the Nazarene, lately organised, is showing great vigour, and gives promise of being a mighty factor in giving Scriptural holiness to the world. Whoever teaches it, or does not teach it, God will have it taught. If any Church that once had the doctrine, backslides and refuses to proclaim it, He will raise up another Church that will proclaim it. Jesus died that He might have a sanctified Church, and the Heavenly Father will see to it that the blood of His only-begotten Son shall not have been shed in vain.

Hymns.

The best hymns of the Churches are full of this longing of devout hearts to be cleansed from all sin. In spite of all the revising of hymn-books to get rid of this doctrine of full salvation, the teaching of sanctification still abounds. The following specimens show it:

> "Rock of Ages, cleft for me,
> Let me hide myself in Thee;
> Let the water and the blood,
> From Thy riven side which flowed,
> Be of sin the *double cure,*
> Save from wrath *and make me pure."*

> "A heart in every thought renewed,
>   And full of love divine;
> Perfect, and right, and pure, and good,
>   A copy, Lord, of Thine."

"Faith to be clean Thou know'st I have
 From sin to be made clean;
Able Thou art from sin to save,
 From all indwelling sin."

"Refining fire, go through my heart,
 Illuminate my soul;
Scatter Thy life through every part,
 And sanctify the whole."

"O come and dwell in me,
 Spirit of power, within!
And bring the glorious liberty
 From sorrow, fear, and sin;
The seeds of sin's disease,
 Spirit of health, remove,
Spirit of finished holiness,
 Spirit of perfect love."

"Breathe, O breathe Thy loving Spirit,
 Into every troubled breast,
Let us all in Thee inherit,
 Let us find the *second rest;*
Take away our bent to sinning,
 Alpha and Omega be;
End of faith as its beginning,
 Set our hearts at liberty."

"Speak the second time, 'Be clean!'
Take away my inbred sin,
Every stumbling-block remove,
Cast it out by perfect love."

"What is our calling's glorious hope
 But inward holiness!

For this to Jesus I look up,
  I calmly wait for this.
I wait till He shall touch me clean,
  Shall life and power impart,
Give me the faith that casts out sin,
  And purifies the heart."

President James A. Garfield, of the U.S.A., was asked by a very dear friend to write in her album. He wrote the following:—

"If the treasures of ocean were brought to my feet,
  And its depths should give up all their coral and pearl,
And the diamonds were brought from the mountain's retreat,
  And with these were put all the wealth of the world,
Not silver, nor gold, nor the gems of the sea,
  Not honour, nor fame, which the world can bestow,
But a *purified heart that from all sin is made free,*
  I would wish for thee, friend, all thy journey below."

This is the universal craving of all true souls, and Jesus can satisfy the craving, through the baptism with the Holy Ghost.

Part 2.
A Review of Keswick Teaching

Chapter VI.
Their Aim. They Teach What we Teach in a Fugitive Way.

AFTER READING MORE THAN SIXTY addresses delivered by the Keswick teachers, we are convinced that they are labouring with us to lift the tone of piety of our time. This is their avowed purpose, and we give them credit for it. We also welcome them and all others who are trying to cast the devils of worldliness and sham and show and self-indulgence out of our Churches, even though they follow not with us. We rejoice with them on the success they achieve. That they have some success we gladly admit. We have met one man who got a blessed experience of sanctification at Keswick, and his life gives ample evidence of it. This brother has abandoned the peculiar Keswick theory and wholly adopted ours; but it is enough that he obtained his blessed experience there.

It is surprising to us and a keen disappointment that we have not met more of such people. This brother's wife went to the Keswick Conventions ten years in succession, and became more and more confused and in the dark on the whole subject. She turned her back on Keswick and its teaching, went to another holiness meeting, and was blessedly sanctified. I have met many such people, both ministers and laymen, male and female, even missionaries. I have met those who went to Keswick on purpose to get the blessing, and supposed they had it. But the wear and tear of life proved that they were mistaken.

I repeat, these things are to me a keen disappointment. What I write is not in any sense personal. I have never met or seen any one of these teachers whose sermons I am reviewing. I am writing by request, and solely in the interest of the truth. If I should at any time seem to be unduly severe, it will be the result of an unfortunate literary style and not any purpose of mine to be unfair or ungracious. To remove from the discussion every element of personality, I will not name the authors of the addresses from which I quote. It is not men but errors that we are combating.

Upon their teachings we make the following observation: It is not difficult to show that in a fugitive and disconnected way they teach just what we teach. For example:

(1) Do we teach *cleansing?* Most assuredly. But listen also to the following from them: "He can save you from an unloving disposition. He can save you from an unforgiving spirit. He can save you from evil desires and inclinations, and from that irritable temper. He can *cleanse* your heart. He can purify your desires. He can control your thoughts. He can transform the whole of your inner being... Come into His presence saying: "Lord, *cleanse* me from every evil way; put me right that I may know the salvation of the Lord."

Again: "There are dark, unclean things which the Holy Spirit may have to deal with in your heart, Christian though you be... They lie at the very entrance into blessing, and until they are confessed and *cleansed* and put away, you cannot live in communion with God."

Again: "So we read, by one offering He hath perfected for ever them that are sanctified, perfected them as to the conscience, giving them a perfect forgiveness, giving them a *perfect cleansing.*"

Again: "There is a mighty river, the river of God's holiness. Oh to get into it. Oh to have that river in us and flowing through us, *cleansing* our thoughts and our desires, *purifying* our thoughts and our desires, *purifying* our whole being. Here is holiness— not a process, not an attainment, but God's precious gift, and He is longing to fill us with that holy life."

Again: "May God *cleanse* our inclinations and desires, and emotions. The Spirit will do so."

Again: "That is what we want— to let the stream of spiritual power flow through our hearts and *cleanse* them."

Now here are six passages that are unmistakeable. But these were all that we found in forty sermons, which took many days to preach. These passages can be read in two minutes. And many other passages in this very Keswick teaching deny utterly the doctrine of cleansing as we shall show.

(2) Do we teach *immediate cleansing,* or sanctification, or deliverance from internal foes? Most certainly. But so do they. Hear this: "He who is able to save to the uttermost, put an end in one minute to eighteen years of misery. And that is what He who can save to the uttermost wants to do with you. You have had eighteen years of weakness; eighteen months of weakness... The Son of God was manifested that He might destroy the works of the devil. He is able with *a word* and with *a touch* to loose you from your bondage, and from your infirmity, and to give you back the upward look, the joyous look into the Father's face."

Again: "When sin is hidden there must be cleansing.

And, mark, the purification of the heart is by faith, not by process. 'Purifying their hearts by faith.' There is an immediate work of God that can remove the veil."

Another says: "A man can be cleansed in *a moment* by the Spirit of God."

Another preacher says: "Our battle is not merely a battle against the weaknesses we find within. It need not be; for, in *five minutes,* that can all be ended. But there are forces without, and the battle with them never ends."

Now these four preachers teach immediate sanctification. But they are flatly contradicted by others, as we shall show.

(3) Do we teach *a second work of grace,* a distinct epochal experience, as marked and as distinct as the first work of regeneration? So do they. Here is a specimen: "In those early years (of Keswick) there were many testimonies of a practical deliverance from the power of besetting sin, a constant and lasting blessing found in the keeping power of Christ, which formed so new and blessed an experience that many spoke of it as 'a second conversion.' Though that phrase was never adopted by the speakers, nor given any official approval, yet it was one quite natural under the circumstances, especially in view of the exactly similar way in which the two blessings came to be received. These Christian people knew quite well that it was by simple faith in Christ, when their own powers and efforts had proved worthless, that the blessing of pardon and peace had been bestowed upon them; and now it was a real repetition of the same steps that brought them *this further blessing*. Again, they were shown that their own powers and efforts had failed, and always would fail, to win them deliverance from the power of besetting sins, just as they had failed for attaining pardon. Again they were shown that in Christ, and in Him alone, there lies the secret of deliverance and victory, even as in Him lay the power to forgive. Again they

were told to commit their case unto the Lord, and, that trusting in Him, the deliverance would be theirs, *even as pardon had been received years before.*

"No wonder then that, with so much alike in the need, in the Deliverer, and in the condition of faith, they should express the blessing received as 'a second conversion,' or more often a *second blessing.'* It was a thankful confession of the very marked and real change effected by this grace of God."

Now this and the other quotations we have made, teach plainly a *second blessing.* But we shall show later that a second blessing is as distinctly denied by others.

(4) Do we teach *the destruction of the "old man" of carnality?* Most assuredly we do. But some of them really teach the same. For example: "If you have got the blessing that the Lord brought you here to get, that 'man' in you is dead, and he is not going to prophecy any more, and in his place, a 'risen man' is going to speak the Lord's message at all costs."

Again: "But what does Elijah say? He does not say, 'Kill all the false prophets.' He says, 'Take the false prophets,' and they took them and brought them to the man who represented God, and Elijah slew them. They brought them and he saw to the death of them. And you will have to bring them to the Lord to be slain. Many of us have tried to slay them, but they have been still alive at the end of all our attempts. Just bring them all to the Lord, and ask Him to deal with every one of them, and ask Him to work that great destruction."

Another says: "When the Comforter has come there is no truce in the war against sin. Shall I tell you why? Because He does not deal with specific things merely. He deals with sin itself (carnality), in the light of the Cross." ... "How strange it is that we should ever forget that Christ is sufficient to cleanse, sufficient to keep, sufficient to satisfy."

But we shall find all this denied elsewhere.

(5) Do we teach that *holiness is a possibility and a duty in this life?* We do. And one of their preachers has this splendid passage: "'He gave Himself for us that He might redeem us from all iniquity, and purify unto Himself a people for His own possession.' The will of God is our sanctification that we should be 'conformed to the image of His Son.' ...Nothing less than that can satisfy the heart of God, nothing less than that ought to satisfy the heart of the child of God, that we should be 'conformed to the image of His Son.' That is fundamental: the New Testament declares holiness to be possible when it declares that it is the will of God for His people. The New Testament declares holiness of character to be possible because it clearly teaches that for the creation of that character, Christ came into the world."

Here is another passage: "But I pray you to remember this, that holiness is not merely a privilege, it is a duty. To fail is to fail of the realisaton of your own life. I mention that only to dismiss it, for it is the lowest argument of all. The most weighty argument is that to fail of holiness is to defame Christ upon the highways and in the city. You name His name, but if your children see in you unloveliness of temper, God help you; you would do better to stop naming His name, and give your child a chance." But, alas! We shall see that this, too, is practically denied, and set at nought.

If such beautiful passages as we have quoted in this chapter were the warp and woof of Keswick teaching, instead of being fugitive and stray scraps here and there, oftentimes immensely lonely for want of company, there would only be one school of holiness— the old school of the Bible, that John Wesley and others have done so much to reintroduce to modern times.

Chapter VII.
Keswick Teachers are not Consistent with Themselves, Nor in Agreement with Each Other.

WE HAVE SEEN IN THE LAST chapter that some Keswick preachers teach:

1. Cleansing from inner sin (carnality, depravity).
2. *Immediate* cleansing.
3. A distinct *second work* of grace.
4. Destruction of carnality.
5. Holiness a necessity and a duty.

We have also intimated that all these things were flatly denied by other Keswick teachers.

(1) One of their teachers was reported as saying: "No man can be free from sin while in the mortal body, which sin must indwell us to the last moment of our lives. Let there be no mistake about that."

Again: "It is simply according to our faith that we receive, and faith only draws from God according to our present possibilities. These are limited by indwelling corruption; and while never needing to sin in the sphere of the light we possess, it is ever taught at Keswick, as in every part of God's Word, that there are, to the very last hour of our life upon earth, powers of corruption within every man which defile his very best deeds and give even to his holiest efforts the nature of sin."

Another said in a sermon: "We shall never be sinless in this world because sin is a coming short of God's glory as well as a violation of His will, but we may be delivered from conscious sin."

Another says: "It is possible to know cleansing in the heart; but, though you have that cleansing, you are not sinless." ...If you say there is no sin in you, you deceive yourself."

Another says: "We do not at Keswick make light of those *depths upon depths of mischief* that lie hidden within us. We are not going to explain them away. Sin wrought them: sin did the damage, and sin's Conqueror must undo it. Do not make light of these things that *remain* when all is put right with God up to our present light. There are yet depths which Christ's mercy and grace will have to deal with."

Now, we might pause here and make a few remarks, and ask a few questions. Here are preachers preaching in the interest of holiness. What kind of holiness is it which is *"not free from sin"* to the last day of our lives? What kind of holiness is it, that these men proclaim, which co-exists with *"indwelling corruption,"* "which always will *defile the very best deeds and holiest efforts* of this life"? What kind of cleansing is it which still leaves *"depths upon depths of mischief* in us" to defile our lives?

God tells us that "the blood of Jesus His Son *cleanseth us from all sin,"* and Jesus is "able to *save to the uttermost."*

Six Keswick teachers endorse, apparently, the Bible, and teach cleansing from indwelling sin. But here are four Keswick teachers who are proclaiming a new kind of holiness— *"corruption"* holiness! *"sinful"* holiness! *"depths-upon-depths-of-mischief"* holiness! With the New

Testament before us, nobody can make us believe that such holiness is produced by the Holy Spirit. No wonder that a Christian woman, going for ten successive years to Keswick to learn how to be holy, and to live so as to please God, became more and more confused until she left in despair, and went elsewhere to get sanctified.

(2) In the last chapter we quoted four Keswick teachers who proclaimed *immediate cleansing* and *instantaneous sanctification.* This is what the Bible invariably teaches. But listen to what others of their number say:

"We shall pass to the work of the Holy Ghost, and see how He *progressively* takes the child of God and separates him from the sin of the world, and *sanctifies him by a process* of inworking."

Another taught: "Secret sympathy with some sin, that is the evil— that is where the danger is. Get into sympathy with Jesus, and you will *grow out* of sympathy with all sin."

Another taught: "We have still further to apprehend that while *perfected in Christ,* our *status absolutely* and *entirely perfect,* there is yet a need of *progressive sanctification* in personal enjoyment of it."

This is good Calvinistic Antinomian perfection, "absolutely perfect in Christ," while one has the corruption of sin in himself. But we may observe that this antinomian, imaginary, theological holiness does not agree with I. Peter i. 15: "Like as He Who hath called you is holy, be ye *yourselves* also holy in all manner of living; (v. 16) because it is written, *Ye* shall be holy, for *I* am holy."

But we will proceed with these disagreements. A Keswick preacher says: "But the sanctification of the Holy Ghost *which is progressive* is a magnificent comfort… I fear that what I am saying will disappoint some who have perhaps for the first time attended this Convention. They will have said to themselves: "I will repair to that holy place, and in a moment I shall be transported into a condition of joy and peace and power... But in regard to the work of sanctification there is never said to be any finality, there is never said to be any completion. Until we pass into the presence of the Lord, we must be living in the power of the Holy Ghost. The Holy Ghost must have all the honour of *a progressive sanctification,* which leads to the final issue of conformity to the image of God's Son."

We should think the heart-burdened people who went to Keswick to get rid *at once* of the constant struggle with indwelling carnality would have been cruelly disappointed with such preaching. People want an instantaneous deliverance from the carnal mind, and, thank God, He can give it to them. "The God of peace Himself sanctify you wholly... and may your spirit, and soul and body be preserved entire, without blame." We do not have to wait until we get to heaven. While we are yet in our "body" in this world, we can be sanctified *wholly* ('holoteleis,' through and through, in every part of our being, "body, soul, and spirit"). And the verb sanctify is in the aorist tense. A great Greek exegete of a university says: "The aorist tense denotes singleness of action, *instantaneous sanctification."* Ellicott says on Paul's prayer, Eph. iii. 14-21: "The aorist tense denotes singleness of action, *instantaneous perfecting in love."* Winer in his Greek grammar of the New Testament says: "In no passage of the New Testament does the aorist express an habitual (progressive) act." The fact is we are sanctified by an *act of God* put forth in an instant of time (as we have shown in chapter iii.), just as we were pardoned in an instant of time. The one is as instantaneous as the other. We grow *in* sanctification and will grow for ever: but we cannot grow *into* it. We are put *into* the state of heart by an act of God *instantaneously.* This is the teaching of the English and Greek lexicons, the Greek grammars, and the best commentators of the world.

Joseph Agar Beet, one of the greatest exegetes of England says: "It is worthy of notice that in the New Testament we never read expressly and unmistakably of sanctification as a *gradual process."*

God wants us to be "conformed to the image of His Son" *now,* and His sanctification is bestowed instantaneously.

But another preacher says: "We should be partakers of the holiness of Christ by a *process* of *gradual sanctification."* We might ask: How gradual is it to be? How many years does God give a Christian to *gradually approach* becoming a partaker of Christ's holiness? Twenty? But a Christian may not live twenty *months,* nor even twenty *weeks,* and God wants us to be partakers of Christ's holiness *at once,* to fit us for service here and heaven hereafter. Nothing less than that can satisfy any true Christian heart. "The fully pardoned *must* long to be fully holy," and they instinctively want it *now.* They do not want to wait until time, or growth, or process of development, or death, or purgatory gives it to them. Neither does God wish them to wait, and no such *"gradual sanctification"* is taught in the Bible.

(3) We showed in the last chapter that a distinct *second work of grace* was taught at least by one of the Keswick preachers as a common experience, in the early years of the Keswick Conventions. This is in perfect harmony with our teaching and with the teaching of the Bible. But listen to these discordant notes from another Keswick preacher: "The baptism of the Spirit is always used in the New Testament with reference to regeneration, and never with what is spoken of to-day as the *second blessing."* ... "When the Spirit came they were born again. As an actual fact of life, it was only when the Spirit came—outpoured in baptismal flood, as the result of the work of Jesus upon the Cross— that these men began to live. They were then baptized in the Spirit, and filled with the Spirit." ... "When they believed, it was the whole Gospel, and the Spirit fell on them straightway. There was no *second*

blessing." This, then represents the normal condition of things under the present dispensation." ... "From that Pentecostal effusion to this hour, the Holy Spirit has guarded the entrance to the Church of Christ, and admitted all its members by its own baptism... "Some persons speak of the baptism of the Spirit as *a second blessing*. They teach that it is necessary to ask for, and to wait for, and to expect this baptism of the Spirit, as something different from and beyond conversion. That is a view utterly unauthorized by Scripture. The baptism of the Spirit is the *primary* blessing; it is, in short, the blessing of *regeneration."* ... "Just as the baptism of the Spirit is never spoken of as *a second blessing,* but always as the initial blessing of regeneration; so, in the economy of God, the filling of the Spirit is coincident with *conversion.* When a man is *baptized* with the Spirit, he is *born* of the Spirit, and is *filled* with the Spirit. *There are many who do not enter into the realization of that blessedness at conversion."... "The filling of the Spirit is indeed an experience far beyond that of which the majority of Christians know anything;* but it is the purpose of God that every child of His should be filled not a year, nor two years, nor ten years after conversion, but at the moment of conversion, and perpetually until the consummation of his sojourn upon the earth." ... "The sealing of the Spirit is identical with the baptism of the Spirit." ... "The anointing which is on the child of God is that which was received at regeneration." ... "It is evident that they needed this *power of holiness* that their lives might be transformed. It is this power that He promised to them when He spoke of the coming of the Holy Spirit (which they all got, and everybody gets at regeneration)." ... "The Holy Spirit must equip the preacher, or preaching will degenerate into lifeless rhetoric or heartless argument." ... "Let all be yielded to the fire and power of the Spirit for cleansing and energy, and the pulpit will be the greatest force in all human life." ... "Life under the control of the Spirit is manifesting the glory of the Master and thus witnessing for Him. For such witnessing the world waits to-day. Humanity, amid its sobbing and its sighing, needs a manifestation of the sons and daughters of the King; and in proportion as the temples of the Spirit are yielded to the Spirit that great need of the race is being met."

We have brought these thirteen quotations together from a work of one Keswick preacher, all of them bearing on the one subject. We venture the assertion that a cruder mass of theological teaching was never brought together in an equal number of words. That great educator and writer! Rev. Asa Mahan, D.D., L.L.D., wrote: "No doctrine can be less Scriptural or more manifestly unscriptural than is this! that all believers are in this dispensation baptized with the Holy Ghost at the time of their conversion. If we compare the actual state of our converts with the revealed results of the 'baptism of the Holy Ghost,' we shall perceive at once that no more absurd notion ever whirled in a human brain than the idea that these converts, or even one in a million of them, have received this baptism."

This theory, that every believer is baptised with the Spirit, is confronted by the following difficulties:—

(1) It is contrary to the well-nigh universal interpretation of Scripture.

(2) The creeds of Christendom teach us that there is corruption and pollution remaining in the heart after regeneration, which must be removed before we are fitted for heaven. Many of the creeds teach what the Bible teaches, that this is done and the heart is cleansed by the baptism with the Holy Spirit. (See my book, "The Cleansing Baptism.") But if, as this preacher says, everybody is "baptized with the Spirit," and "sealed with the Spirit" in regeneration, what is left of Divine help for the soul to look forward to for betterment? The poor heart strug-

gling with the carnal mind, the remaining corruption, must fall back upon its own efforts and growth. It would be in vain to call on the Spirit for help, for He has already done His work. Indeed our author says: "*The Spirit is never given in answer to human asking!*" This contradicts Jesus, Who said: "If ye then, being evil, know how to give good gifts unto your children, how much more shall your *heavenly Father give the Holy Spirit to them that ask Him?["]*

(3) These conflicting utterances are like the Midianites stampeding before Gideon's trumpets; they cut themselves to pieces. Notice: "Everybody is 'baptized with the Spirit,' 'filled with the Spirit,' 'sealed with the Spirit,' and 'anointed with the Spirit: in regeneration and conversion." But, "There are many who do not enter into the realization of that blessing at conversion! The filling of the Spirit is indeed an experience far *beyond that of which the majority of Christians know anything!*" In other words everybody gets these stupendous Pentecostal experiences in conversion, but the great majority *do not realize it or know a thing about it!* I should be afraid that if I could get such a treasure as the Pentecostal blessing, God's greatest gift this side of heaven, and not know it, I might lose it and never miss it.

It reminds me of Lorenzo Dow's description of the teaching of Calvinism:

> "If you seek it, you can't find it,
> If you find it, you won't know it,
> If you know it, you haven't got it,
> If you get it, you can't lose it,
> If you lose it, you never had it."

But our author proceeds with the most entirely unconscious inconsistency, to tell us that the Holy Spirit must equip the preacher, or preaching will be worthless, and he exhorts them: "Let all be yielded to the fire and power of the Spirit for *cleansing* and *energy,* and the pulpit will be the greatest force in human life," while he has spent two hundred pages in telling them that *there is no second blessing,* and every thing that is to be had of the Spirit is received at conversion! Again he say: "The Spirit makes witnesses for Jesus, and "for such witnesses the world waits today. Humanity amid its sobbing and its sighing needs a manifestation of the sons and daughters of the King." But if this theory were true that every Christian received the filling of the Spirit at conversion, every Christian would be such a witness. Yet not one Christian in a thousand is such a witness, which proves his theory untenable.

As another illustration of the Keswick contradiction, this preacher says: "The Spirit is never given in answer to human asking." But another says: "You are not going to get filled with the Holy Ghost until you have got down on your knees. It is in answer to prayer that God fills with the Spirit. He giveth the Holy Spirit to them that ask Him. He will be enquired of for this thing, and He will have you in earnest, definite, constant petition until you get your answer."

How strange to listen to such contradictions from the same platform.

Chapter VIII.
Painfully Indistinct Teaching at Keswick.

My introduction to this teaching at first hand was through a book, the title of which is, "Holiness by Faith: A Manual of Keswick Teaching." It contains four addresses by four prominent Keswick preachers. I read it through twice very carefully that I might not be unfair in judging it. After two readings I wrote this comment at the end:

"This is a strange book. The preface says the aim is to give plain instruction on the doctrine of Holiness by Faith. Yet the word 'holiness' is in the book only fifteen times, aside from the top of the pages; the word, 'holy' only in seven places; while the word 'sanctification' is used only once. Nothing is said of the baptism with the Holy Spirit for heart-cleansing, or of Pentecost, or of Christian Perfection, or of Perfect Love. No example in the entire book is given of anyone who professed to obtain 'holiness by faith.' No clear direction is given '*how to obtain it.*' There is a suggestion of condemnation at professing it. A thousand men with seeking hearts might read the book and not one get the blessing."

I then studied over sixty sermons in various volumes of

The Keswick Week. I say nothing against the ability of the sermons, or their interesting character, or their eloquence, or style. I am not concerning myself with such matters. I am only considering them as bearing on the subject of holiness, which they profess to teach. I am free to say that many of them had no particular relation to the subject. For spirituality they were not a whit above the average of multitudes of sermons preached everywhere by men who do not dream of thinking that they are preaching on the subject of holiness.

The first sermon I read had this passage: "Your life will be illuminated. An illuminated life is a holy life." This was the only passage in the sermon that by noun, adjective, or verb even hinted at the subject of holiness.

The next sermon had the phrase, "Wholly and happily yielded up to God," and this was the solitary suggestion of anything bearing on the subject of holiness. The next sermon did not have a word that even suggested that subject. The next sermon had ten blessed lines which we have already quoted. It was the only passage in four entire sermons that pictured heart-cleansing, or would let anyone have the slightest idea of what anyone should endeavour to obtain. The next sermon had not a line in it advocating an experience above regeneration. There was not a sentence from beginning to end teaching sanctification or holiness, or pointing the way to it. The next sermon did mildly and indefinitely approach the theme, and would have awakened serious thought on the subject. The next one was interesting and showed an orator's skill: but it did not teach holiness, either what it is or how to get it. The next sermon had holiness for its theme; but it was indefinite, and too vague for anyone outside the experience to understand. Furthermore, it had a passage, near the close, positively unscriptural.

The next preacher chose one of the best texts of the Bible for preaching the great doctrine that Keswick professedly stands for. I was compelled to write at the close of it: "A fine opportunity missed; no description of the evil that afflicts our moral being, how we got it, how it affects us, or how to get rid of it."

I soon came to another sermon which was much better in tone and more Scriptural. It really taught the death of the "old man," under the philosophical figure of identification with Christ on His Cross. It would have been simpler and vastly more easy to understand if the speaker had taught that on the Cross provision was made for the death of our "old man," if we will have it so, by the baptism with the Holy Spirit, through faith. It was blindly stated, but it means just what we teach. These preachers continually make the impression that they are restrained from referring to the baptism with the Holy Spirit as the remedy for carnality. The next sermon did try to teach sanctification; but it taught it as a *progressive* work, confounding purity with maturity, and was neither clear nor Scriptural.

Another sermon was most interesting and able; but as I read it I was compelled to write: "Only inferentially bearing at all on the subject of holiness, which was not mentioned. Would men, if utterly unhelped, be at all likely to draw the inferences?" The truth is, the carnal heart is very blind to spiritual truth. Paul declared that the god of this world had blinded the minds of those who were perishing. It will not do for preachers to be so misty. They have a commission to men "that they may turn them from darkness to light, and from the power of Satan unto God, that ye may receive remission of sins, and an inheritance among them that are *sanctified* by faith in Me (Christ)." Multitudes of preachers themselves do not know the truth of full salvation. The writer himself preached for twenty-three years while a stranger to it. When a preacher does get a heavenly vision of the truth, and enters into the experience of holiness, he has no right to veil the truth by obscure words. He must declare it explicitly with no uncertain sound. This is why God so signally honoured him with the heavenly light, that he might clearly illuminate others and help them to holiness of heart and life. We have been listening to holiness preaching now for a dozen years by our holiness evangelists in the United States. In their preaching there was no such vagueness and indefiniteness. And when we read these Keswick discourses we are at once amazed at the utter lack of lucidity in many of them. We cannot help asking ourselves how men preach sermons at a Holiness Convention so utterly vague and nebulous. Some of them do not even hint at the subject they are supposed to teach.

We came to another sermon which, if we may judge from what we have read, was the author at his best. It had in it a real call to holiness in these words: "Shall we take our rights this morning then, and, cost what it may, face the majesty of God's holiness, and as He calls you, His conscious agents, through the help of human beings, to be holy because He is holy, how dare you trifle with the world and go back and lust after the flesh-pots and cucumbers, and leeks, and onions of Egypt?" Then later comes a call to consecration as follows: "It is God that asks that you should give Him back, in gratitude, yourselves, your soul, body, time, talents, money, possessions. They are not yours at all; you are only going to say, 'Thank Thee, Lord; take back Thine own.'"

That is beautiful, and what everybody must do to be sanctified. But there he stopped. Why, we cannot imagine. That is only *consecration* for sanctification, the *human condition* of getting the blessing, and *not the blessing itself.* But after consecration, still another human condition must be complied with, namely, *faith.* We "receive the Spirit by *faith.*" We are "*sanctified by faith.*" Our hearts are "cleansed by *faith.*" Now, after giving the Scriptural call to holiness, and inviting to *consecration* for it, how could the preacher have missed urging his audience to exercise faith for the blessing then and there? We have but one explanation to offer: he teaches a *gradual, progressive sanctification.* With such nebulous teaching we do not wonder that many hungry-hearted people go year after year to Keswick, and come away as mystified and as hungry as ever.

I turn the leaves and read the comment at the end of another sermon: "Not one word pertaining to holiness in this sermon." After another was written: "Just at the close of this sermon, the preacher vaguely reached the truth in two lines." I then came to another sermon, at the close of which I had written: "A beautiful sermon about the Holy Spirit; but it was indefinite. There was no direction as to how to obtain the fulness of the Spirit, or what to seek." We remember that in the early years of our ministry, before we knew anything about this great subject, we preached a series of nine sermons on "The fruit of the Spirit." I never heard afterwards that anybody got the fruit. Undoubtedly my sermons all had this characteristic vagueness. I did not then know myself how to receive the Holy Spirit in baptismal fulness and power, and how could I teach others? Is it possible that a similar difficulty affects many of the preachers of these sermons? We sincerely hope not; but these amazing facts confront us, and there is some explanation of them.

At the close of another sermon we were compelled to write: "He approached the subject once in this noble sermon; but then he receded. He comes to the witness-stand, but does not testify." Another is described as: "Like a bugle-call to action, but no holiness in this sermon." At the close of another sermon on "Peace," we wrote: "Strange that he did not say that peace in the soul came by deliverance from the carnal mind, which is always at war with all good." How could anybody who knows the source of the "peace of God which passeth all understanding" miss telling it to an audience? After another we wrote: "This is a beautiful sermon. If in all his eight sermons he had only told them even once to repair to the Pentecostal chamber and stay until the cleansing Spirit came! But he did not, and was strangely indefinite."

I will make only one more of these comments. One preacher said in his last sermon: "There are scores of people in Keswick to-day who cannot hear plainly what God speaks because of a habitual unbelief, and their testimony has been wrecked. They have nothing to say. They cannot say: 'God has done *this* for me,' because they have not put Him to the test." But there was not one paragraph in his seven sermons to indicate what *"this"* refers to, or to show what a person was to believe for, or to try to have God do.

Chapter IX.
Much that these Preachers call Holiness is Only Regeneration.

LET US NOT FORGET the discussion of regeneration and its definition in the second chapter. The Bible standard of regeneration, as we have said, is a life of OBEDIENCE. "Whosoever is begotten of God doeth no sin, because His seed remaineth in him: and he cannot sin, because he is begotten of God. In this the children of God are manifest and the children of the devil: whosoever doeth not righteousness is not of God" (I. John iii. 9, 10).

We have quoted this definition of regeneration: "Regeneration is that moral change in man wrought by the Holy Spirit, by which he is saved from the love of sin, the practice of sin, and the dominion of sin, and is enabled, with full choice of will and the energy of right affections, to love God and to keep His commandments."

Both the regenerated man and the sanctified man are alike held to strict and cheerful obedience to every known will of God. The difference between the two is not in their *outward conduct* so much as in their inner *state of life.* The regenerated man finds in himself the "remains of inbred corruption" or "remaining pollution" as a TENDENCY to pride, anger, envy, or any other form of sin. But the sanctified man is cleansed from this corruption, so that he has a "pure," or "sanctified," or "holy" heart. "The blood of Jesus Christ His Son cleanseth us from all SIN": "sin" in the singular number, the sin principle. In sanctification the Holy Spirit cleanses the moral nature from the pollution of depravity. This is *Scriptural holiness.*

Now, bearing this distinction between the regenerated and the sanctified man in mind, it will be seen that much that is called "holiness" by Keswick teachers is only the obedience of regeneration. Notice these quotations: "Do not be afraid of being too perfect. There never will come a day in your life in which you are not conscious of being very imperfect. But that is not what I am specially referring to. What I am speaking about more particularly is this: God pointing out to you, at the beginning of this Convention, that there is something wrong— something that is inconsistent with your position as a Christian; are you willing to give it up?"

Now, we do not see how anybody could either *get* regeneration or *keep* it without giving up everything that he knew to be wrong. But the result would not be holiness.

Again we quote: "The heights of the absolutely holy will always tower above us in the blue sky: but in spite of all, we may BE KEPT FROM KNOWN AND CONSCIOUS SIN. In the holy sight of God, and judged by His perfect standards, our best will be full of infinite deficiency, but *up to the measure of our knowledge* we may walk before Him in holiness and righteousness all our days."

The reader will notice that in this closing passage of an eloquent sermon, not a thing is said about having a *"pure"* heart or a "clean" heart; but being "kept from known and conscious sin," and obeying God "up to the measure of our knowledge" is held up as holiness. The attention of the audience was wholly turned to the outward *doing* and not to the inward *state of heart*. And this correct *conduct* was called by the preacher "holiness." But this, as we have seen, is only genuine, Scriptural REGENERATION.

Here is another Keswick preacher: "The special mission of Keswick is to promote a Scriptural standard of holiness. To this it has devoted itself for more than thirty years. It is important to ask what is God's standard of holy living. 'Can I do no sin?' you say; in one sense you can. You can commit no known sin. There is a great deal of sin, you may be sure, that you commit that you do not know. It is absolutely atrocious that a child of God should step on the platform of sin when he knows it to be sin."

There was great confusion of thought in that quotation about the nature of sin against God which we will pass by. But here is a distinct announcement that the Keswick platform teaches that "Scriptural holiness" is only refraining from the COMMITTAL OF "KNOWN SIN."

We do not hesitate to say that this utterly misses the Scriptural idea of HOLINESS. If it were, then the only synonym for "holiness" would be "obedience." But why, then, does God say so much about a "pure heart" and "a clean heart," and about "purifying" and "cleansing" and "purging" and "circumcising" the heart, by "removing" something from it, and "taking away" something, and "putting off" something, and "crucifying" and "destroying the body of sin," and "making dead," and "sanctifying," and "sanctification"? Away with an interpretation of Scripture that brushes aside with a wave of the hand this tremendous array of expressions which all teach HEART CLEANSING, and substitutes for them all *outward obedience*, and avoiding "conscious sin"!

Here is a quotation from another sermon: "When will we be done fooling with sin? There is nothing more appalling about sin than the fact that it tempts even the saints to trifle with the deadly thing. God has two great words, 'Repent,' 'Forsake': that is repentance. 'Lay hold': that is faith. 'Hold fast': that is perseverance. These three cover the whole territory of our experience." ... "There is that kind of sinless perfection in which every Keswick teacher believes: the sinless perfection of instantaneously and forever renouncing every known sin." Now this is some more of the same bad theology. It simply holds up regeneration, and calls it "holiness." But we flatly deny that repentance, and faith for regeneration, and perseverance *"cover the whole territory of our experience"* We can bring ten thousand humble witnesses to testify that after they sincerely repented of sin, and believed for pardon and regeneration, and faithfully persevered in the same, walking in the light as God gave it to them, they were convicted by the Holy Spirit of their need of A CLEAN HEART. With great heart-hunger they went to Jesus, consecrated all their ransomed powers to Him, and all their good things to be the Lord's forever. They pleaded for Jesus to baptize them with the Holy Spirit for a holy heart. In simple faith they claimed the blessing. The Spirit came, and wrought a cleansing in their heart, and gave them the experience of sanctification, as clear, as distinct, and as marked, and as definitely witnessed to by the Holy Ghost, as was their conversion. I believe there are thousands of people who could testify to such an experience this minute.

The following is taken from another sermon: "If there is anything for which Keswick has stood for thirty years, it is for the necessity of obedience in order to light, in order to blessing. Not one of the teachers on this platform has ever winked at disobedience in any form, or given any soul any comfort while continuing in disobedience, and it is taught here consistently that obedience must be a studious obedience, that looks at little as well as at great things... Disobedience is deadly. It tends unto death. It tends to the decay of all spiritual affections, and spiritual convictions, and spiritual sensibilities, and spiritual choices. Whether you are a child of God or not, at once stop your disobedience. Turn your back at once on everything sinful or doubtful if you want to walk in the light."

This is well said. I do not complain of it. I am only saying, it is not all that the Scripture means by "holiness" of heart. It is only the experience of regeneration, as the Bible pictures it. *The lowest state of grace in God's Word is a life of obedience.*

One other passage of this kind ought to be sufficient to prove what I am saying, that most of these preachers teach only a *regeneration experience* for holiness. Here it is: "Just walk right out on the divine promise (he does not tell which one), trust it absolutely, trust it for the SUBDUING OF SIN, trust it for the answering of prayer, trust it for the dispersion of darkness, and the triumph of faith will be VICTORY OVER INIQUITY."

Here, then, is the largest hope and the most exalted privilege held out to a believing child of God by this preacher; it is to have the indwelling SIN WITHIN HIM "SUBDUED," and have "VICTORY OVER INIQUITY!" The reader will see that this is only regeneration as God describes it in the verses quoted at the beginning of this chapter.

Is this the highest privilege of God's child to have the indwelling sin only *"subdued"* and repressed, but still left within us, to torment the life? Even this preacher cannot quite make himself believe it; for in another sermon he accidentally staggers onto the truth after this fashion: "It seems as though the disease of sin were so desperate that it has invaded the psychic centres of our being, paralysing the mind and heart and conscience and will with its terrific power... While there is a spiritual sense of the law of God, there is a carnal slavery to the law of sin." ... "Be sure you come to the Great Physician. The devil is a quack. His methods are abnormal; they are palliative but not curative. When he sees you have got a deadly disease, instead of applying the knife and cutting out the cancer, he applies a palliative." ..."I think the Lord as a Physician uses very drastic and decisive measures in dealing with the disease of sin. Like a skilful physician, He has four measures:— First, the DESTRUCTIVE measure: as when the physician uses the scalpel, the lancet, the cautery, to DESTROY SOMETHING like a cancer or tumour. Secondly, the PURGATIVE: as when cathartics or emetics are used to cleanse the system of something that is deadly in its influence."

Hallelujah! What an oasis of truth this is in the midst of such teaching! "DESTRUCTIVE measure" of treating the disease of sin! "PURGATIVE measure" to cleanse from the moral being the "deadly" carnality! "CUTTING OUT THE CANCER" of the carnal mind which is enmity against God!

Why, brother! That is what the other holiness teachers are proclaiming all over the world, that Jesus Christ can "cleanse" out, "purge out," "burn out," "destroy" the "body of sin," by the fiery baptism with the Holy Spirit. We tell sorrowing, dissatisfied, sickly Christians that the Great Physician has a "CURATIVE" treatment that can rid us of the disease of sin altogether. But this is contrary to the whole trend of Keswick teaching.

It is for the blessing of real, inward holiness that the heart of every believer longs:—

"Lord Jesus, I long to be perfectly whole,
I want Thee for ever to live in my soul;
Break down every idol, CAST OUT EVERY FOE:
Now wash me, and I shall be WHITER THAN SNOW. "

"O for a heart to praise my God!
A heart from sin set free;

A heart that always feels the blood
So freely shed for me:

A heart in every thought renewed,
And full of love divine,
Perfect and right and pure and good,
A copy, Lord, of Thine.["]

Chapter X.
Unsound Philosophy about Self, and the Nature of the Flesh or Depravity.

MY ATTENTION WAS CALLED TO the unsound philosophy of some of the Keswick teachers about "self," by some thoughtful people, before I had read a single sermon preached from that platform. I was told, also, in the same conversation, of some who speak about dying to "*self*" and "the death of *self*," till it becomes little better than refined Buddhism. A careful reading of more than sixty of these addresses convinces me that the criticism, in some instances at least, is just. According to the lexicon, "self" means "one's own individual identity," "one's own person," "personality," "individuality," "personal identity."

In their discussions "self" is often substituted for indwelling sin or depravity. I read this from a Keswick preacher: "The *flesh* is 'self' spelt backward. It is '*me.*'" Again, "Self is the pivot around which the natural man revolves. It is the essential principle of every sin, and has been ever since that *first sin* in which Adam preferred what was pleasant to the eyes and calculated to make him wise, to the will and word of God. Sin is the assertion of *self*."

Another says: "Have you ever said to your sinful self—that self that cannot be improved, that self for which there is no healing medicine except death— have you ever said to that sinful self, 'My sinful self, thou hateful thing, breaking out now in pride, and now in passion, and now in jealousy, and now in indolence, and now in selfishness, breaking out in a thousand hateful forms; my sinful self, I put thee, where the sinless Christ put thee on the Cross: hang there, for God put thee there?' "

Another quoting Matt. xi. 28 says: "The burden is *self*. And every human being in this tent at this moment is living a God-centred or a self-centred life; there is no other burden possible."

A preacher quotes Rom. vii. 24: "O wretched man that I am! who shall deliver me from the body of this death?" and interprets it to mean, "Who shall deliver me from" *myself?* "Who shall save me from myself?"

Another sentence reads: "Man made self the centre rather than God, and herein our race fell."

I could quote a half-dozen other passages of similar import, but these are quite sufficient. Now I do not believe this is either sound philosophy or the thought of Scripture. It is very confusing, and no ordinary audience would get any help from it. Indeed, it is doubtful if *any* audience would, for no natural meaning can be put to this language that will make it harmonise with either fact or Bible truth, as the following observations will make evident:—

(1) If the word" flesh," when used in the bad sense, as by Paul, means "me," then Jesus loved it; for Paul says, "He loved *me* and gave Himself for *me*" (Gal. ii. 20).

(2) If "the flesh is 'self' spelt backwards," why did Paul write to Timothy: "Exercise *thyself* unto godliness. Take

heed to *thyself* and to thy teaching. Continue in these things; for in doing this thou shalt both save *thyself* and them that hear thee." It seems that Paul thought "self" was something to be saved, not something to be despised and destroyed

(3) If "flesh," used in the bad sense— that hateful thing that opposes all good— is self, why did the great apostle write to the Corinthians: "Let us cleanse *ourselves* from all filthiness of flesh and spirit, perfecting holiness in the fear of God"? The word "flesh" here does not mean anything but our body, and "flesh and spirit" mean "self"— the whole of us. It is not "*self*" that we are to be saved from, but the "defilement," "filthiness" of self, that needs to be cleansed away. Then "self" would be holy.

(4) If "flesh" is "*self,*" "*me,*" why did the apostle John write: rt Every one that hath this hope set on Him (Jesus) purifieth him*self,* even as He is pure"? This apostle seemed to think that there was an abnormal condition from which the *self* only needed to be purified, and then it (the *self*) would be *pure* as Jesus is pure.

(5) If the flesh is "me," and that is what they mean by the "sinful self"— that self that cannot be improved, that self for which there is no healing medicine except death— then death itself would bring no relief, for death cannot save a man from himself. The *self,* whatever it is— character, record and all, passes right over into the next world, like a man moving from one house into another across the street. There would be nothing to offer any sinner, indeed any of us, according to Keswick teaching, but annihilation. So the Nirvana of Buddhism is the sole hope of us all!

Now if, on the other hand, we were to interpret their term "sinful self" to mean the "old man of indwelling sin," the "depravity of our nature," the "bias to evil," which must be, and may be, put to death now, and leave us pure and holy, we could understand it. But this is exactly what they all along deny— that the Holy Ghost can kill the "old man" of "indwelling sin." But without this interpretation there is not a glimmer of sense in all this talk about "me" and "flesh" and "self" and "sinful self."

(6) One asks, "Who shall save me from *myself?"* and represents that to be what St. Paul meant when he said, "Who shall deliver me from the body of this death?" That is not within a million miles of what the apostle meant. He was, in vivid language, in the first person, representing not his own experience at that time, but the experience of anybody struggling with carnality. What he wanted was not "deliverance from *himself,"* but he wanted *himself* delivered from *carnality.* When a man has an inflamed and pain-stricken eye, he does not want his eye dug out and annihilated. The eye, as God made it, is all right: it is the disease, the *inflammation* that needs to be removed. When a man has ear-ache, it is not the ear that he wishes to have destroyed, but the *abnormal condition* of the ear removed. When the magnificent arm of an athlete has blood poison, he does not want his arm amputated; he wants the poison removed. So the cry of a depraved soul is: "O wretched man that I am! who shall deliver *me* from this depravity?" The answer comes at once: "I thank God (I have deliverance) through Jesus Christ our Lord" (Rom. vii. 25)·

Bishop Ellicott says: "The 'old man' is the personification of our whole *sinful condition* before regeneration," and we add "after it, too." Our nature, our "self," as God made it, is all right: but the *sinful condition* needs to be removed. There is an abnormal element in us injected by Satan, which is no essential part of our being. It is the *sinful condition.* When that is removed man's *self* is again an image of God.

(7) One of these preachers says: "The self-life is not something that is to be improved, or repressed; the self-

life is something that is to be terminated, brought to an end." The "old man" is the "former self." Now let us see. The "former self" was composed of body, soul, and spirit plus sin, or body, intellect, sensibility, and will plus indwelling sin. And this former self, "self-life," he seems to say must be brought to an end. This is annihilation again! Why not use intelligible Bible language, and say that *sin* is to be cleansed out of us, leaving the *self* pure and holy, as God originally made it.

(8) One says: "Self is the pivot around which the natural man revolves. It is the essential principle of every sin, and has been ever since that first sin. Sin is the assertion of self." This is not true either in morals or philosophy. Men have to assert themselves to resist tempters and temptations. "My son, if sinners entice thee, consent thou not." "Resist the devil and he will flee from you." What is that but self-assertion? If Adam and Eve, while they were holy, had asserted themselves, they would not have gone down in shameful defeat.

Perhaps this preacher meant by "self," *selfishness* as "the essential element of sin." But even that would not have been sound philosophy. Let us hear from a teacher of my young manhood, that lucid thinker, Prof. James A. Fairchild, who treats of this subject in his "Moral Philosophy" as follows:—

"Wrong, or sinful action, is the action which we morally condemn, and for which we pronounce the agent blameworthy. It is a refusal to meet the obligation or duty, a refusal to be benevolent, or to will the good of being as in itself valuable. It is, of course, unreasonable action; for reason presents happiness, well-being, as good, and benevolence, or the choice of that good, as duty.

"Sinful action is opposed to reason and intelligence, and must find its motive elsewhere than among the facts and considerations which reason presents. Its sinfulness consists in *the refusal to be benevolent*— the duty ever present to the moral agent. But unreasonable action must have a *motive*— an inducement to refuse a choice so excellent and praiseworthy. The motive to wrong action is found in the impulse of the desires and passions. These have their seat in the sensibility, and, when aroused, solicit the will to seek their gratification, even at the sacrifice of good and the claims of duty. The man, in the exercise of his freedom, has power to yield to these solicitations, neglecting the claim of duty, or to refuse to yield; and in this choice he determines his moral character. Yielding to desire or passion as his controlling motive, he becomes a sinner. The desire terminates on some object, some relative good which excites desire, and the attainment of which tends to gratification. The immediate aim of the action to which desire impels is the attainment of its object. But it cannot properly be said that the object of desire is the motive. It is the motive only as it awakens desire: that desire itself is the immediate motive. The object may be really useful, a means of good, as contemplated by the intelligence, or it may be in the end harmful, pernicious, and known to be such: it matters not so long as desire fastens upon it. The inebriate, mad with the love of drink, quaffs the poison, even though he knows that at the last 'it biteth like a serpent and stingeth like an adder.' Desire is blind to the good or evil, on the whole, that there is in the object. It operates upon the will by its own blind force as an impulse, and not by considerations of interest or value. Thus *motives to sin come through the desires and passions,* while *motives to virtue appeal to us through the intelligence and reason."*

"In all forms of sinful action the sinful element is the same, the neglect of well-being, the refusal to be benevolent. Apart from this element there is no sin in gratifying desire… The gratification of desire is to be accounted as good, to be held as a part of universal well-being subject to the claims of duty, the decisions of reason. Here was the failure of our first parents. When they 'saw that the tree was good for food, and that it was pleasant to the eyes, and a tree to be desired to make one wise,' they took of the fruit, while *duty*, as indicated by the divine command, and their own reason as well, forbade the eating. This was the nature of the first sin in our world, and has been the characteristic of every sin from that day to this. Without such a command, and without any apprehension that the eating was improper, the gratification would have been indifferent or even a duty. There is no sin in mere pleasure or enjoyment; the sin is in the unbenevolent choice which is involved in the acceptance of the pleasure.

"We have seen that *virtue involves obedience to reason and intelligence,* and *sin involves subjection to the desires and passions"* (pp. 29-31). In the same vein, my theological teacher, Dr. Samuel Harris, of Yale, taught us that *"Sin is the refusal to obey the dictate of right reason."*

President Fairchild continues his discussion on "Wrong Action or Sin," maintaining that "sin is not selfishness," as follows:—

"It is still more common to represent *selfishness* as the fundamental sin; probably because selfishness seems, in its nature, so directly opposed to benevolence, and benevolence is virtue. In this view selfishness is defined to mean the choice of our own good, as the supreme end, while benevolence is the choice of all good. This representation supposes two possible ultimate ends of action—the good of all, the choice of which is benevolence or virtue, and our own good, the choice of which is selfishness or sin.

"The evil-doer, on this view, is pursuing, as his supreme end, his own good. Pursuing this end, he must bring all his resources into service, and call upon his intelligence to devise ways and means to promote his own happiness, so far as calculation and wisdom can compass it. He will not sacrifice a greater good in the future to a present indulgence; for this is opposed to his supreme end. He will not confine his attention to this life, if he has any evidence that there is another, because thus he would sacrifice his own interests. If he has reason to believe that the favour of God has more to do with his welfare than that of any other being, he will be most diligent to secure that favour. If he learns that honesty is the best policy, and that benevolence, virtue, is the truest source of satisfaction, he will give himself with all his soul, to an honest and virtuous life; and if he does not do this it will be because he is ignorant of the fact that blessedness comes with virtue. Thus, selfishness, in the sense of making one's own good supreme, must, in the end, annihilate itself. In fact, it is only from ignorance that it can ever exist. It is from the beginning only a blunder. The truly selfish man, in the sense above defined, a man seeking his own highest good, needs only to learn the good which comes from benevolence, and he becomes virtuous at once, because his well-being requires it.

"If it be said that he cannot become virtuous for such a reason, I answer, then he cannot seek his own highest good as his supreme end, because that end requires him to become benevolent; and, if he refuses, he relinquishes his end— ceases to pursue his highest good.

"We have reached the conclusion, then, that it is impossible for a finite moral being to pursue his own highest good, or his own good at all, as his supreme end. In such a pursuit he must take intelligence as his guide, otherwise he does not pursue the end proposed at all: and one of the first facts which reason offers to him is that benevolence is essential to his happiness, and benevolence is the choice of all good as the supreme end.

Thus he ceases to pursue his own good as supreme, and relinquishes his end in obedience to that end itself—

a *contradiction which is inevitable upon the theory that sin is the pursuit of one's own good.*

"The doctrine is equally at fault when viewed in the light of the evil-doer himself. That he is not pursuing his own good as his end is manifest on the slightest consideration. One of the most notorious facts of sin is that it is utterly opposed to the interests of the sinner. In its most promising and successful forms, it is confessedly a sacrifice of the greater interests to the less. The sinner, in his best estate, aims at some worldly advantage, and fails of the life to come. He seeks some temporary pleasure, and foregoes the higher joys of a virtuous and benevolent life. Even if we confine our attention to material, worldly good, the lower forms of satisfaction, we find few who have sufficient self-control to surrender an insignificant present enjoyment to a greater future good. 'A little sleep, a little slumber, a little folding of the hands to sleep,' is the cry of the sluggard, while 'his poverty comes as a robber, and his want as an armed man.'

"We come no nearer the truth to say that the sinner thinks he is pursuing his own interest. He has no such thought. He sees, when he gives attention to his case, as those around him see, that he is his own worst enemy—laying snares for his own feet, plotting his own ruin. You would not insult the drunkard by asking him if he follows his best judgment in reference to his own welfare. Your hope of recovering him from the way of death is in the fact: that his own judgment condemns his course as ruinous. He knows, as no other one can know, that the seeming good that he pursues is an illusion and a lie, and yet he is not persuaded to renounce his folly and accept substantial good...

"If it be said that sin is the choice of self-gratification as an end, the doctrine is not materially altered... The sinner sacrifices his own gratification, even as he apprehends it himself, to his appetites and passions. No one has ever doubted that a well-regulated life brings with it more gratification even of the bodily appetites than a course of unrestrained passion. If they pursued self-gratification as an end they would act more wisely…

"The only sense in which the sinner lives for himself is that he regards not his rational self but his *physical self*, the animal, or rather sentient, nature, made up of the desires and passions. Here he finds his motives to action, and thus lives a life of impulse and not of reason. The name by which St. Paul designates this state is not *selfishness* but *carnal-mindedness*— caring for the *flesh*, a term which expresses with philosophic accuracy the nature of the action. By the term *'flesh'* he means not merely the *bodily appetites*, but *the aggregate of the desires and passions*, of which the bodily appetites are the most conspicuous.

"Let it not be forgotten that the sin is not in the desires and passions themselves, nor even in their gratification, but in the constant refusal to accept the good as the aim of life. The desires and passions are the motives which induce this refusal. The desires and passions are a part of our constitution, given us by the Creator, but given to be controlled and not to control. We are rational beings, and the truths and realities, in view of which we ought to act, are presented by the reason.

"If it be asked, Why are these impulses given us, since they furnish temptation to sin and are the sources of all evil? it may be replied that they are the condition or channel of all good as well as evil. Without them we should be as valueless as dead matter; our being would be nothing in itself, and useful only as there were other beings endowed with desires who could use us. It is through the sentient side of our nature that all precious things exist to us, and the broader and deeper and more various these susceptibilities and wants, the higher we stand in the scale of being. If the desires be eradicated as the occasion of sin, the possibility of virtue ceases at the same time. It is only required that we set the limit to our gratifications which duty enjoins, sacrificing no good to impulse or desire." ("Moral Philosophy," pp. 33-37.)

One can plainly see from the above how very inexact and loose and faulty is the teaching of Keswick about "self." The flesh is not "*self*" or "*me,*" but only a part of self, and, in the bad sense, it is the *diseased condition* of self. It is not true that self, or even selfishness, is the essential principle of sin, as the moral philosopher has shown. It is not true that it is a virtue to disregard self, or a sin to have concern for self. Jesus Himself made the proper love of self a duty and a virtue when He said: "Thou shalt love thy neighbour as *thyself.*" We are a sacred creation, made by God for His glory, with faculties like His own. Even our bodies are fearfully and wonderfully made, marvellously adapted to be the present home of the soul. They who speak lightly of it as the source of evil are in imminent danger of blaspheming its Maker—God. The body, erect and admirable, strong and beautiful, is the fit instrument of the spirit through which man operates upon the forces of nature around him, and becomes acquainted with his environment. Through its eyes he sees the beautiful; through its ears he hears the varied voices of nature. He becomes acquainted with the qualities of things through its power of touch and taste and smell. More sacred than any Cathedral ever made, it even becomes the temple of the living God. Add to this body our intellectual and spiritual faculties and we become wonderful beings, only a little lower than the angels, and crowned with glory and honour.

All the powers and faculties of this being are sacred, and should be sacredly guarded and kept for holy uses. Mistaken teachers advocate a "death to self," and then to intensify it, add "a deeper death to self." We know of no people in the world so absolutely "dead to self" as the vilest sinners. They are even dead to the sacred laws of health of their own bodies; they pervert their appetites against the instincts and protests of nature. They violate all the laws of well-being by deliberate courses of profligacy and vice. Women are often dead to health and modesty in matters of dress. Sinners are dead to the voice of reason and the protests of conscience and the demands of self-interest. They are dead to their own deepest wants and highest hopes and holiest inspirations. They are dead to present welfare and future good; so dead that having eyes they see not, and having ears they hear not the things that make for their eternal peace. They see not the shame of their own moral nakedness, and see no beauty in personal holiness that they should desire it. They are so deaf that they hear no call of duty and no command of God.

Be dead to self! No, let us be evermore seriously, solemnly *alive* to the dignity of our being, and the nobility of our relationship as the sons and daughters of the Most High. Let us train our bodies and minds and hearts that we may be fitted for the noblest service for God and man and for the highest eternal destiny. Whether we eat or drink, or whatsoever we do, let us do all to the glory of God.

Let us lay ourselves at Jesu's [*sic*] feet for the cleansing of our whole being, and then arise and shine in the likeness of God.

Chapter XI.
The Practical Issue.

My task is nearly done. I have written in great seriousness. My heart has been most solemn as I have set forth the errors of Keswick teaching. I do not impugn the motives of these teachers, or their character, or their good intent. I profoundly hope they are a world better than their theories. I think undoubtedly some of them are. Religious teachers often get befogged by their theology, and teach utter vagaries which time and investigation explode, while their hearts are right with God.

I again remind my readers that I have studiously avoided all personalities. I am a stranger in a strange land. I have never met any one of these men whose teachings I have reviewed. I probably never shall have the honour of meeting them in this world. Hitherto, at least, our lives have moved in different orbits: our paths have never crossed. I have no conceivable motive for criticizing their teachings except in the interest of TRUTH which is sacred to us all, and in the interest of the Kingdom of Christ to which we have given our lives.

I am assured, and am glad to know, that occasionally one gets sanctified in their meetings. But that does not prove that, as a whole, their doctrines are in harmony with the Bible, any more than the fact that Madam Guyon got sanctified, proves that all the doctrines and abominations of the Roman Catholic Church, of which she was a member, are of God. She got sanctified in spite of the doctrines of her Church as a whole, and not on account of them; and so people may occasionally get entirely sanctified through Keswick influences, in spite of the general trend of the theories and doctrines there held and taught.

But we have proved to a demonstration by quotations from their own writings:

(1) That Keswick teachers are not consistent with themselves, nor do they agree with each other. So far from it, in a most astonishing way they contradict themselves and contradict each other. This is a great hindrance to those who are trying to arrive at the truth.

(2) We have shown that their teaching was painfully indistinct This is a great fault in any public teacher, and it usually arises from a want of clear knowledge of the subject on the teacher's part. Clear thought begets lucid utterance.

(3) We have proved from the Bible, and by numerous quotations from them, that what Keswick teachers call holiness is only regeneration. We are delighted if they gather a great mass of unregenerated or backslidden Church-members at Keswick annually and get them regenerated. But when they call the standard of obedience, which they hold up, "holiness," they inflict a grievous wrong upon the dear children of God already regenerated, who are there seeking a holy heart. They also inflict a great wrong upon the cause of holiness, and it must certainly grieve the Holy Ghost.

(4) We have shown that they have substituted "self" for "sin" (indwelling sin-depravity) and then have resorted

to a very confusing and unsound philosophy, to teach their views.

Here is a tender story which teaches its own lesson. It needs no comment or emphasis from me.

"A young lady moving in high social circles in a distant land was convicted by the Holy Ghost of her need of salvation. She trusted God to forgive her sins for Jesus' sake, and, realising that her past was under the blood and her name written in heaven, with the witness of the Holy Spirit in her heart, she walked in the path of obedience to the known will of God.

"Her outward life was right, and only in the heart was there any difficulty in giving glad obedience on every point when light was given. But a great hunger for inward purity led this loved sister to ask leading Christians if there was any better experience than the new birth. No one was able to help her; but England was suggested as the place where it was likely the experience longed for might be found.

"Determined to get God's best, she reached London in time for the May meetings, and was diligent in her search after holiness of heart. Right through these meetings she was an earnest seeker, but found not the blessing she sought. She was advised by friends to stay till the Keswick Convention came on. She did so, and reached that famous place more hungry than ever for that satisfaction which Jesus said should come to those who hungered and thirsted after righteousness.

"Her expectations were great, and as thousands of people were gathered to hear from godly preachers how to get the blessing referred to by Jesus in Matthew v., she fondly thought that her appointed time had come. The Convention was almost over. Many meetings had been attended with longing desire for what the people called the Keswick blessing; but no light from heaven had reached her soul. Many precious statements of truth were made. Many helpful messages were given. But the one desire of her heart for inward cleansing was unrealised, and satisfaction was still to her an unknown experience.

"The Convention was over, and the leaders and the throngs were leaving. Her heart was so sad and her hopes were so shattered that she was in agony, and she went out alone and cried unto God for the help she so much needed. Observing a meeting of some kind in reference to Pentecost announced, she asked her friends what kind of a meeting it was; and she was warned not to go, as the Pentecostal League, under whose founders, Mr. and Mrs. Reader Harris, these meetings were being conducted, taught the possibility of sin being eradicated instead of being suppressed or counteracted, as the Keswick platform does.

"Too anxious for the deliverance which the Keswick teaching had not given her, she determined to hear for herself whether these things were so. In the very first meeting God showed her, through the messages inspired by the Holy Spirit, that what she needed was the baptism with the Holy Ghost. Gladly she obeyed God's call, and, trusting in Him, she received the blessing.

"Now she knew what it meant to be cleansed from all sin, including heart sin, and to be filled with the Holy Ghost. God has blessed her witness to many others, and some who have been blessed through her testimony are in the very front ranks of real holiness work to-day. Her own statement was that *the Keswick preachers did not teach real holiness, but only a good regeneration experience."*

Beloved Keswick preachers, here was a typical case. God awakened in a regenerated heart a great hunger for holiness, and sent her fifteen thousand miles to you that she might receive the blessing, and you were so handicapped by your theory that you were powerless to help her. I assure you, she is only one of a multitude of deeply pious souls who come to your Convention to get a clean heart, and they come away more hungry and more sad than when they came.

I have been in this country but five months and I have met many of them. How vast must the whole number be!

If there was not something radically wrong in your teaching it would not, *could* not, be so. You belittle the nature of the *uttermost salvation* which Jesus bought for us with His blood. You lower it to the level of the obedience of regeneration. You make nothing of the indwelling or heart-sin, the raging propensity to evil; or if you mention it, you teach that it is only to be suppressed. You thus belittle the cleansing power of the blood of Christ and the baptism with the Holy Ghost. Indeed, the *latter* you seldom mention, or direct people to seek. Yet it is the one cure of their heart-longing, the one remedy for "the carnal mind," the one power that can destroy "the body of sin," and leave the moral being cleansed, and pure and holy.

Does it never occur to you that it is too late in the Christian centuries to invent a new kind of holiness? Mighty-minded, Spirit- illuminated men, filled with the Holy Ghost, bent reverently over the Sacred Page and discovered the truth about holiness long ago. We do not need any new theory; we need to have the old theory applied. The Gospel that made St. Paul and his assistants holy, "cleansing their hearts by faith," is good enough even for this twentieth century. The Gospel that made Wesley and Fletcher and Carvosso and Adam Clarke and Asbury such heavenly-minded men, and made them such prodigies of Holy-Ghost power, will answer the needs of to-day.

Above all, when men and women hunger for the Bread of Heaven, do not offer them a stone. When, Spirit-led, they long for deliverance from the carnal mind, and pray in agony of soul to be made pure in heart and sanctified and holy, do not, we beseech you, mock their sorrow by offering them a holiness which is not a complete cure for the whole disease of sin.

Chapter XII.
Closing Words.

When men turn from the path of Scripture truth and begin to speculate on a subject, agreement is at an end. Harmony may no longer be expected. Their past theories will be found untenable and new ones must be invented, which are quite as worthless, to take their place. In turning from the plain teaching of the Holy Word, Keswick has not escaped this inevitable result.

At the Keswick Convention of 1912 one of the speakers publicly renounced the doctrine of the suppression of inbred sin as unscriptural— what they had been teaching at that Convention for thirty years— and substituted in its place the equally unscriptural term "counteraction." He did not, however, say in what passage of the Bible the word is used in reference to depravity.

Now we submit that "counteract" does not mean "purge away," "take away," "put off," "purify," "destroy," "crucify," "free from," "eliminate," "root up," "mortify," or "annihilate." All of these words are given in the Greek lexicons as definitions of the verbs that describe the Divine cure for carnality.

The absurdity of this new Keswick notion will appear if we substitute these terms, "counteraction" and "counteract," for some Bible terms. We will write the Scripture verses, putting the new terms in parenthesis after the old: —

Isaiah i. 25: "I will purely purge (counteract) away thy dross, and take away (counteract) all thy tin."

Ezek. xi. 19: "I will take away (counteract) the stony heart."

Ezek. xxxvi. 29: "I will save you (counteract) from all your uncleanness."

Mal. iii. 3: "He will sit as a refiner and purifier (counteracter) of silver, and He will purify (counteract) the sons of Levi, and refine (counteract) them as gold and silver, that they may offer to Jehovah offerings in righteousness."

I. Cor. v. 7: "Purge out the old leaven." How insipid to say, "Counteract the old leaven"!

I. John i. 7: "The blood of Jesus His Son cleanseth (counteracts) us from all sin." How weak and unbiblical this new reading sounds in these grand passages!

Heb. xiii. 12: "Wherefore Jesus also, that He might sanctify (counteract) the people with His own blood suffered without the gate." How repulsive to the ear and to the mind!

Heb. ix. 26: "He hath been manifested to put away (counteract) sin."

I. Thess. iv. 3: "For this is the will of God, even your sanctification (counteraction)."

Heb. x. 10: "By the which will we have been sanctified (counteracted)."

Acts xv. 9: "Purifying (counteracting) their hearts by faith."

II. Cor. vii. 1: "Having, therefore, these promises, beloved, let us cleanse (counteract) ourselves from all defilement of flesh and spirit, perfecting holiness (counteraction) in the fear of God."

Rom. vi. 6: "Knowing this, that our old man was crucified (counteracted) with Him that the body of sin might be done away (counteracted)."

Rom. vi. 22: "But now being made free (counteracted) from sin, and become servants of God, ye have your fruit unto sanctification (counteraction) and the end eternal life."

Now, what a shabby substitute this new theory is for the incisive, radical words of God! It makes many of these Scriptures grotesque, and reduces others to absurdity. Well does the great writer say, "What fools these mortals be!" How hard men strive to dodge God's plain and blessed truth that promises complete deliverance!

We are aware that very able physicians sometimes use counter-irritants to draw inflammation from some inner vital part of the body that is seriously diseased, and cannot be directly reached by remedies. A case in point came to us a few months since. More than half-a-century ago an American youth studied for two days so laboriously on a mathematical problem without sleep that he ruptured a blood-vessel in his head and became unconscious. Counter-irritants were used to draw away the inflammation and brain disturbance. As a last effort his breast was repeatedly burned with a hot iron. But it succeeded. Bear in mind, IT SUCCEEDED! The boy lived to become a hero of the Civil War. He had three horses shot under him, and fifteen bullets go through his clothes and hair. He became a major-general, a governor of the State, and is still living a ripe, honoured old age. From his own lips we got the story!

But Keswick offers no cure. It offers only a perpetual counteraction for a life-long disease of indwelling sin. It might be fitly symbolised by the perpetual burning of the back of the neck with a hot iron to relieve an unrelievable, incurable, cerebro-spinal meningitis! Depend upon it, the mighty Healer of Nazareth and the Sanctifying Spirit have a more satisfactory and a more immediate cure for the malady of inbred sin. They invite us to receive the fiery baptism with the Holy Ghost that will burn out carnality and purify the heart. (See Acts xv. 8, 9).

One of the oldest and most honoured of the Keswick leaders has written a little booklet on "The Blessing of Cleansing." In it he tries to uphold and elucidate this new counteraction theory. He gets himself into the following logical muddle:—

Fact No. 1: *"Sin,"* he says on p. 10, *"is not an essential element in the constitution of our humanity.* We know that it was not in man originally, nor will it be in man as finally glorified; neither did it exist in the Man Christ Jesus." This is true and Scriptural.

2.— He tells us that sin exists in different forms.

(1) As an offence against God," "a transgression of law," "a rebellion against the Sovereignty of God" (pp. 12-14).

(2)" Sin exists as a ruling principle" (p. 16). *"Sin is a power that has entered into the central citadel of a man's being, and, establishing itself there, has brought every part of his nature under its sway." "Sin is a principle that is essentially opposed to God"* (p. 17). "The believer sees that Christ, by dying for him, delivered him from sin as a ruling principle. *Its power is broken.* He in that sense is 'free from sin'" (p. 19). But this death of Christ in itself alone is no "freedom from sin" and no "cleansing" at all. Christ died for every sinner in the world; but that fact alone does not "free him from sin" or "cleanse" him. The sinner is still full of sin, and the believer may still be full of "the sin principle."

(3) "Sin exists as a moral defilement" (p. 20). "But we may be separated in heart and mind from the defiling influence of sin" by "the committal of our whole being to

Him for this blessing" (p. 26). The author does not tell us how it is to be done, whether by "suppression," or "counteraction," or "eradication," or "cleansing."

(4) "There is sin as a spiritual disease" (p. 26). "Christ has come to open the prison doors— to burst the fetters that keep the soul in slavery to sin" (p. 30). This, too, is true, but the author does not tell us whether the disease is salved over and "counteracted" and still left lurking in the system, only a bit "suppressed," or whether it is banished, purged out, by perfect health.

(5) Sin as an acquired habit" (p. 31). "We are not born with habits, though we inherit that which gave rise to them." "We are born with the *sinful tendency,* but we are not born with the sinful habit. Every evil habit may be entirely laid aside; but this does not mean that *the tendency to sin is thereby eradicated*" (pp. 32, 33). On pages 36-38 he denies that the tendency to sin can be taken away. "There are some who seem to maintain that the blessing of being 'pure in heart' is a *state* of purity, rather than a *maintained condition* of purity. The distinction is important" (pp. 37, 38).

The author then gives two illustrations. "A light taken into a dark room dispels the darkness. Let the darkness represent sin and the light represent holiness. When a light is introduced into a dark chamber the darkness instantly disappears, but the tendency to darkness remains; and the room can only be maintained in a condition of illumination by the continual counteraction of that tendency" (p. 39).

Now this illustration utterly fails in this respect[.] He has told us on p. 17 that sin is a fearful malignant "*power that has entered into the central citadel of man's being.*" But darkness is no "*power.*" It has no "*tendency.*" It is *nothing,* a mere *negative;* simply the *absence* of light.

Then he takes another illustration which is still more unfortunate. "When a balloon with a car attached to it is ascending from the earth its tendency is upward" (p. 45). "Suppose we say the weight of the materials of which it is composed, or, in other words, its tendency downwards, is equal to four, and the lifting power of the gas with which it is filled is equal to six. As these two forces are diametrically opposed, the power by which it actually ascends is only equal to two" (p. 46). The weight represents the tendency of sin; the uplifting power of the gas represents Christ. He *counteracts* the natural tendency to sin."

This illustration signally fails in this respect. Weight in the balloon cannot represent sin; for weight is an *essential quality or element* of matter. But he told us on page 10 that "sin is not an essential element in the constitution of our humanity. It was not in man originally, nor will it be in man as finally glorified; neither did it exist in the Man Christ Jesus." The subject of this dear man's booklet is "The Blessing of Cleansing." But he tells us of no *cleansing* at all. The "tendency to sin" is still left in us to foment evil habits. Sin and holiness are dwelling together in the same heart. We are "free from sin" only in the sense that the "power of sin is broken." But it may get mended some day, in fact any day, and upset the life!

Now, why does this educated Christian man write such logical crudities and contradictions, giving illustrations that do not illustrate, and describing a cleansing that does not *cleanse,* and offering us a Saviour Who, he declares, is not able in this life *to save* us from the tendencies and propensities to sin that continually defile the Christian life? There is only one explanation: he was arguing against the plain, simple truth of the Word of God, and no man living can do it and be logical. He never mentioned the purifying "baptism with the Holy Ghost and fire," nor "sanctification," nor the provision of "the blood of Jesus Christ that cleanseth us from ALL sin." He flatly contradicted Scripture by teaching that we could not be cleansed from sin as a tendency in this life. That means that *death* must do it: and so death is mightier than Christ and the Holy Ghost!

Still another Keswick preacher teaches another kind of holiness— the old Calvinistic "IMPUTED righteousness of Christ" and "finished salvation." Said one preacher at Keswick:

"The perfection of *standing* we do not have to go on to; we are in that; the perfection of position is ours now. In Jesus Christ, in the sight of God, I am just as perfect as Abraham and Moses and David, with their harps before the throne— absolutely perfect in Christ in standing and position."

We have heard of this kind of sanctification before— "Sanctification in *standing,* but not in state. We are already sanctified by our *standing* in Christ." Those who thus teach, with one accord reject sanctification as an *"experience"* or *"state,"* because they do not need it. They already have a *"sanctifying standing in Christ."*

We will quote a few pages from the Calvinistic writings of the past to show to what horrible excesses and conclusions this monstrous doctrine had led. "Every elect vessel, from the first instant of his being, is as pure in the eyes of God from the charge of sin as he shall be in glory. Though such persons do act rebellion, yet the loathsomeness and hatefulness of this rebellion is laid on the back of Christ; He bears the sin, as well as the blame and the shame. And God can dwell with persons that act the sin, because all the filthiness of it is translated from them upon the back of Christ… A believer may be assured of pardon as soon as he commits any sin, even adultery and murder. God does no longer stand displeased, though a believer does sin often. There is no sin that ever believers commit that can possibly do them any hurt. Therefore, as their sins cannot hurt them, so there is no cause of fear in their sins committed… Though I believe David's sin displeased the Lord, must I therefore believe that David's person was under the curse of the law? Surely, no. Like Ephraim he was still a pleasant child, though he went frowardly (in adultery and murder), he did not lose the character of the man after God's own heart. The elect are "justified from all things" even before they believe. In all their sins God views them "without spot or wrinkle or any such thing." "They stand always complete in the everlasting righteousness of the Redeemer. Black in themselves, they are comely through His comeliness. So that when they commit adultery and murder, He "Who is of purer eyes than to behold iniquity" can nevertheless address them with, "Thou art all fair, my love, my undefiled; there is no spot in thee." ... "For His glory God often permits His own dearest children to commit adultery, robbery, murder, and incest to bring about His purposes. He has always the same thing in view, namely, His own glory and my salvation, together with that of the other elect. This Adam was accomplishing when he put the whole world under the curse; Onesimus, when he robbed Philemon, his master; Judah, when he committed incest; and David, when he committed adultery."

(1) It will be seen at once how such teaching naturally leads to Antinomianism, and away from the experience of true, experimental holiness. One who is elected can do what he pleases and still have "a sanctification of standing in Christ." David may commit adultery and Solomon may be wallowing in vileness in his unparalleled harem, and building temples of idolatry for his heathen wives, and Peter may be cursing and denying his Lord, yet, according to this Calvinistic teaching, and the preacher I quote, they are all "just as perfect in the sight of God as Abraham and Moses with their harps before the throne," "absolutely perfect in Christ in standing and position"!

(2) It will be seen how utterly unscriptural such teaching is. God says: "Be ye *yourselves* also holy, for I am holy." No fictitious "sanctification of *standing* or *posi-*

tion," without experience in the heart, is at all acceptable to God.

Another Keswick preacher at their Convention held up the Seventh of Romans as a picture of St. Paul's best and maturest life, and concludes: "You cannot, therefore, honestly deny that there are these two laws, even in a saintly life." A young man came out of the service saying, "That is the best sermon on holiness I ever heard." That young man, under the influence of that deceptive, misleading sermon, undoubtedly got that kind of holiness at the Convention. He will spend the year groaning: "I am carnal, sold under sin. O wretched man that I am! Who shall deliver me from the body of this death?" And he will go back to the next Convention to hear again of the Seventh of Romans holiness!

Years ago we heard a course of sermons in Willard Hall, Chicago, at noonday. One day the speaker took a photograph of this man in the Seventh of Romans: "His camera the Word of God." THE SHARP DETAIL of this man shows he is powerless to do good (v. 19), whereas a (sanctified) Christian is enabled to be perfect in every good work (Heb. xiii. 21). EXPOSURE: This man exposes his position by saying: "I am carnal, sold under sin (v. 14), and not spiritual" (Gal. vi. 1). DEVELOPER: This man develops a body of death (v. 24) and not a body which glorifies God (I. Cor. vi. 19, 20). FIXING: This man has fixed himself under the law and is brought into captivity (v. 23), and is not as yet under grace (Rom. vi. 14). THE NEGATIVE: The negative of this man of Rom. vii. now shows: "I," 28 times; "Law," 21 times; "sin," 16 times; "Me" and "My," 17 times; "Dead," 8 times; "Death," 5 times, AND NOTHING OF CHRIST (see Gal. ii. 20). TONING: When toned down the image shows he is a "wretched" man according to his own statement (v. 24), whereas a sanctified Christian is always rejoicing with joy unspeakable and full of glory (I. Peter i. 8). PAPER PRINTING: This man printed out shows he serves the law of sin (v. 25), but a sanctified Christian is dead to THE sin (Rom. vi. 2) and is freed from THE sin (Rom. vi. 18-22 and Rom. viii. 9). The preacher said: "I am sorry to see that many Christians take shelter in this chapter to excuse their condition, and seem to think this state is the mark of humility. If you are like this, may God help you. Do not dishonour Jesus by upholding this to be a Christian experience— 'carnal, sold under sin.' I would rather call myself a heathen than use this expression." Yet this doleful chapter that records the experience of Paul or some other man as a Jew under conviction, trying to get saved and sanctified by *law,* describing in graphic language his bitter bondage to THE SIN dwelling in him, and the despair it brought, is held up at Keswick, not only as a Christian experience, but as the best experience of the ripest saint of the Christian ages!

The truth is, while unsanctified Christians do have some of the same struggles with the carnal mind that are depicted in this chapter, yet *the chapter, as a whole, is the picture of a convicted sinner,* and the Early Church so held for four hundred years. Thirty-two of the leading modern commentators have gone back to the early interpretation.

It is in the eighth chapter that St. Paul gives his up-to-date experience. Here he tells the astonished Jews and the world what Jesus did for him. He unfolds the power and virtue of the Gospel scheme. It pardons and sanctifies. The law could do neither. This picture is so totally different from that described in the preceding chapter that it is absolutely impossible that they should be the description of the same man at one and the same time. *There* he was a wretched captive, tugging at his chains; *here* he is free. *There* he was trying to save himself; *here* he is already saved by another. *There* he was groaning; *here* he is shouting happy. *There* it was agonizing prayer; *here* it is rapturous praise. *There* he was defeated ; *here* he is victorious. *There* it was dark despair; *here* it is cloudless hope. The two experiences are absolute, irreconcilable contradictions, mutually exclusive.

Again, to a thoughtful observer there is a wide discrepancy between the inspiring songs and earnest prayers of some and the preaching of others. At the opening of a service they sing:

> "O for a heart to praise my God,
> A heart from sin set free,
> A heart that always feels the blood
> So freely shed for me!
>
> A heart in every thought renewed,
> And filled with love divine;
> Perfect and right and pure and good,
> A copy, Lord, of Thine!"

Then a precious brother prays: "Destroy the evil within us, and cleanse us from all that is unlike Thee, and make our hearts, 'perfect and right and pure and good, a copy, Lord, of Thine.' Let us be filled unto all the fulness of God. Bring our hearts into perfect harmony with Thyself. Anything unlike Thee take away." Then a man will preach that there is no such blessing or experience possible for us in this life! The Saviour cannot save to the uttermost, nor His "blood cleanse from ALL sin." The "O wretched man" experience is the best there is, and the best that was ever lived in this world!

At another service a good brother prays that "the Holy Spirit may come upon them in Pentecostal power, and burn out of their hearts all pride and envy and jealousy and unholy temper and passion and lust, and make them like Christ." They sing a song which is nothing but a prayer for the Holy Ghost.

Then a brother preaches who has published in a pamphlet that it is a mistake to pray for the coming of the Spirit, and God never taught us to do it!

What would honest inquirers think of such conflicting teaching and such jangling voices?

We circulated among the Keswick visitors for days, and thought it was the most hungry, earnest, teachable, and, we are compelled to add, the most confused and bewildered and befogged audience we ever saw. The reason is that the leaders are dodging God's great truth of full salvation, and of course in their human speculations there can be no harmony.

The Greek language must be re-formed and the Greek New Testament re-written and the Greek Lexicons made over, before much of the teaching of the Keswick platform can be true. Thank God, the baptism with the Holy Spirit can *thoroughly burn all the dross of sin out of the heart;* Christ can save to the *uttermost;* and *His blood can cleanse from all sin,* Keswick to the contrary, notwithstanding.

This last chapter has been written at a later date, and in the interval the writer has attended the Keswick Convention.

www.ingramcontent.com/pod-product-compliance
Lightning Source LLC
LaVergne TN
LVHW010623100826
845148LV00014B/3083

9780880196314